Table of Contents

For Will

Foreword

Many years ago, when I was a child of four or five years old, I saw a picture of the *Dai Butsu*, the great statue of Buddha that has stood in the town of Kamakura, Japan for more than 750 years. The picture I saw was an illustration in volume three of a set of *Golden Book Encyclopedias* under the heading for Buddha. And although I came from a Catholic family and knew nothing of Buddhism until much later in life, that picture beckoned to me. I had the feeling that someday I would go to Kamakura to see that great statue...And one day, I did.

My journey to Japan began in the town of St. Helena, California, in the heart of the Napa Valley, where I was the proprietor of a small tailoring business. One spring afternoon, Mark Raus, a man I'd met at an Oktoberfest celebration a few months earlier, came into my shop with some clothing in need of repairs. I was newly single and so was he, so when he asked me go with him to the symphony in San Francisco, I said yes. On our date, he told me of his travels in Europe, and of his desire to embark on another adventure, this time to Japan. He had a friend who was there teaching English in Tokyo.

Over the next few months, our relationship blossomed, and the next thing we knew, we were 35,000 feet over the Pacific Ocean, on a 747 bound for Narita Airport. Little did I know just how profoundly that journey would shape the rest of my life. Upon our arrival in Tokyo, Mark's English-teaching friend Bruce Whistler extended us his generous hospitality. Within two weeks of our arrival, we were both employed as full-time English conversation instructors at Gakken White House, and shortly thereafter, we found a furnished apartment that we could afford on our salaries. In the two years that followed, we spent our afternoons and evenings teaching English in a conversation salon, and our weekends and vacations seeing as much of the country as our time and budget would allow. And of course, our very first outing was a visit to the *Dai Butsu* at Kamakura.

An unexpected detour in our Japan adventure occurred when I discovered that I was pregnant. But instead of hightailing it back to the States, we decided to stay and have the baby in Japan. This turned out to be a wise and wonderful choice. There was a rainbow over Tokyo the day our beautiful baby boy was born. We named him Will. And although Mark and I have now gone our separate ways, we remain friends and dedicated parents to our son. Our lives have been irrevocably etched and will always be defined by the experiences that we shared in that remarkable culture.

My time in Japan left an indelible imprint on my life. The simple act of waking up each day was filled with possibility…countless opportunities to observe, to learn, and to be inspired. In Japan, one need only move through the day with a mindful eye, a willing spirit, and an open heart. And among the thousands of experiences I enjoyed during my stay, these are the ones I remember most fondly.

Gomen Nasai

Before I went to Japan, I was already familiar with the culture and had studied the two basic alphabets, however I only knew how to speak a few words of the language. My vocabulary consisted mostly of *kudasai, arigato,* and the names of my favorite kinds of sushi. But I had neglected to learn any of the practical phrases that would get me through an average day. And when preparing for the trip, I tried to pack light but still ended up with several large pieces of luggage; and I insisted on bringing my guitar, although I never played it that often.

When we landed in Japan, my companion and I took the Keisei Skyliner from Narita Airport to Ueno Station in Tokyo, with our eventual destination being the home of a friend who lived way out in the suburb of Oji. The trip required several train changes, and each time a train stopped for us to board or debark, we had to quickly transfer our two sets of luggage from the platform onto the train, or vice versa, in the few seconds before the doors closed again and the train took off. It was touch-and-go at every junction, but we had managed so far to successfully board the final train with all of our luggage in tow. Just one more stop and we'd be home free.

When the train finally pulled into Oji Station and the doors slid open, I was poised to make my move. Without looking,

I heaved my oversized suitcases onto the platform. Little did I know that a diminutive Japanese businessman was waiting just a little too close to the door, and I bowled him right over with my luggage. Never before or since, have I been at such a loss for words. I was mortified. Of course I helped him up with many a chagrined apology in English, but what I wouldn't have given in that regretful moment to have known how to say, "*Gomen nasai!*" ❖

Déjà vu

On many occasions throughout my life, I've had premonitions that come to me in dreams. On the way to Japan, on a stopover in Honolulu to soak up a little tropical sunshine before resigning ourselves to the February chill that awaited us, I dreamed of the apartment that would eventually become our home away from home in Tokyo. In my nocturnal fantasy, I saw two rooms separated by a sliding panel, the apartment was fully furnished, the proprietor was a Japanese woman, the rent was $350, and it had a piano! Of course, we both had a good laugh the following morning when I described the dream. All that, and a piano too, for less than half the price of a walk-up flat in San Francisco…Preposterous! Everyone knows that rent in Japan is astronomically expensive, and apartments are so small that the futons have to be stored in closets to make use of the floor space for other activities during the day. A Technicolor dream indeed.

But as destiny would have it, we only looked at one apartment in Tokyo, and that's the one we rented. It was located in a fairly modern, two-story building in Nishi Ikebukuro, in a quiet neighborhood about ten minutes' walk from Ikebukuro Station. The proprietor, Mrs. Motoko Koyama, a lovely but high-strung Japanese woman, met us at the west exit of the station and guided us to the address.

I felt a chill run down my spine when we arrived at the apartment and discovered that the main living area consisted of two rooms: a large, combined living room and kitchen, and a smaller *tatami* room, separated by a sliding *fusuma* panel. And I could almost hear the spooky theme song to *The Twilight Zone* when I saw that the place was fully furnished with futons, a low table, a refrigerator, a gas heater, a washer, a sewing machine, and…a piano! A black lacquered Yamaha upright, just like the one in my dream. The apartment rented for ¥90,000, which, at the time, when converted to U.S. dollars, was equivalent to about $700, making my half of the rent…about $350. I guess some things are just meant to be. ✤

Next Stop: Pandemonium

The transit system in Tokyo is massive and labyrinthian, and it is jam-packed to capacity and beyond at rush hour every day, with millions of bustling businessmen and women scurrying to and from their offices. The express trains are especially crowded because they travel at faster speeds than the local trains and don't stop at every little station along the way. But whether it's an express train, or a local train, at rush hour, the platform attendants literally have to pack the passengers into the train cars so that the engineer can get the doors closed. When the train arrives at its destination and the doors open again, those same people, propelled by their urgency to escape the breathless confines of the over-packed train, burst forth onto the platform in frenzied droves.

During my search for a job in Tokyo, I was still staying out in the remote suburb of Oji, where the Keihen Tohoku Line that services the area is far less crowded than the inner-city trains. To get to my job interview in Shinjuku, I had to transfer to the busier Yamanote Line that encircles the city of Tokyo. The train I rode in on was crowded, but not intolerably so, and I arrived at my interview right on time. Afterwards, I returned to Shinjuku Station to catch the train back to Oji. I had just come through the turnstile near the stairs leading up to the platform that services the Shinjuku Express, which, as coincidence would have it, had just pulled into the station.

Witnessing the debarkation of the express train at Shinjuku Station is one of the most harrowing experiences on earth. It's a veritable *tsunami* of humanity, most of them Japanese businessmen dressed in blue suits and white dress shirts, all of one mind: getting to work on time. In their haste, they sweep across the train platform and down the stairs, barreling over anything and anyone in their path. In that instant, I saw a wall of people coming down the stairs, and before I could find my feet to make a run for it, I was in the very midst of that stampede. For the next two minutes, I watched in dismay as no fewer than two thousand people trampled past, not one of them taking any notice whatsoever of me, pinned to the wall, paralyzed with fear. Fortunately, a narrow vertical column sheltered the spot where I was standing and saved me from being knocked off my feet. Then, in a twinkling, just as quickly as it had begun, the whole incident was over. The frantic commuters had jostled through the turnstiles and vanished into the streets of West Shinjuku, leaving me a little dazed, but thankfully unscathed.

I got the job, by the way. And when I learned that my workday would begin each afternoon at two, and would end each evening at ten, I breathed a sigh of relief just knowing that I wasn't going to have to join the world's worst rat race after all. ❖

Soroban

Japan is a paradox of ancient traditions and modern devices coexisting within a single society. It's not unusual to see an *Edo*-style temple standing next to a contemporary office building, or a crew of field workers, ankle deep in water, planting a rice paddy with high-rise buildings reflected in its mirrored surface. One day, while standing on the train platform waiting for the express train to Shinjuku Station, I witnessed my favorite paradox of all.

The train platforms in Japan typically have a kiosk that sells sundries such as newspapers, cigarettes, umbrellas, souvenirs, candy, snacks, and beverages to busy commuters. Another convention in Japan is the use of the abacus, which the Japanese call *soroban*, as means of calculating figures. Postal clerks, shopkeepers, and even some bank tellers use them in the course of everyday transactions. School children learn the basics of the abacus, but to use one professionally requires a skillful technique, almost like playing a musical instrument. Therefore, many Japanese people take special, advanced classes to learn how to use an abacus properly.

What, you may ask, do a train platform kiosk and an abacus have to do with each other? Well, on this particular day, while standing on the platform at Ikebukuro Station, waiting for the express train to take me to my job in Shinjuku, I spotted an old woman, the proprietor of a sundries kiosk, bent over a computer-generated spreadsheet printed on that familiar green and white striped, accordion-folded paper with the perforated edges. I didn't think anything of it at first. She was just an old Japanese woman in an apron, perhaps doing her monthly bookkeeping. But upon closer observation, I realized that she was checking the rows and columns of figures on the computer spreadsheet…with an abacus! ❖

At Long Last

The Taiisan Kotokuin Shojo Shrine in Kamakura Japan is my very favorite place in all the world. It is the site of the great bronze statue of Buddha known as the *Dai Butsu*, and within a few weeks of getting settled in Tokyo, we chose it as the destination for our very first outing. On a lovely Sunday afternoon in early spring, we boarded a train on the Yokosuka Line at Shinagawa Station, bound for Kamakura. What we hadn't counted on was, at precisely that moment, three thousand other people had exactly the same idea. Before we knew what was happening, we found ourselves crammed into the portico between two train cars, and the doors slid shut for the fifty-four minute trip. There were no fewer than a dozen people sandwiched into that narrow passageway, and this being my first experience with traveling under such claustrophobic conditions, I was terrified. Throughout most of the trip, I tried to quell my panic and endure the ride. But at each station, as the train drew nearer to Kamakura, more and more people got on, and no one seemed to be getting off. Finally, at Kita Kamakura Station, just one stop from our destination, I was literally ejaculated from the train when a number of passengers made an *en masse* exit. Feeling the glorious freedom of unlimited space around me, and breathing the first easy breath I'd drawn in nearly an hour, I suddenly decided that there was no way I was getting back on that train, even if I had to walk all the way back to Tokyo.

I planted myself obstinately on the gravel shoulder next to the tracks while Mark stood in the doorway of the portico, trying his best to reason with me. "It's only one more stop," he said in a quietly rational tone of voice. "And look, no one is getting on, there's plenty of room now." Just before the doors closed again, he finally convinced me that I would survive the remaining half-kilometer to Kamakura station; and so, reluctantly, I got back on the train: A decision I have never regretted.

Although for reasons I don't fully understand, seeing the Dai Butsu for the first time was one of the most profound moments of my life. I'm not sure there is a word that would do it justice, yet, if pressed to give it a name, I would have to say that it was the massive serenity I felt in its presence. All one hundred and twenty five bronze tons of it, an overwhelming magnetic force, a vortex of tranquility. In that moment, there was nothing else: no crowded trains, no hustle and bustle of Tokyo, no greedy, busy world, no strife, no anger, no hatred, no war…only an abundant and abiding peace. I was home…Om.

And so, there it sits, as it has for more than seven centuries, the Dai Butsu at Kamakura, quietly dominating the lush landscape that surrounds it, drawing countless thousands of troubled souls unto itself, perhaps to impart a small yet enduring pearl of that same peace, a moment of stillness to carry always within. ❖

Before and After

The transit system in Japan is an essential and integral part of everyday existence. With more than 100 million people relying on it for both commute and recreational travel, it is the lifeblood of all commerce. Locations of any kind are typically identified first by the transit line on which they can be reached, and then by the nearest train station. Throughout my stay in Tokyo, I lived near Ikebukero Station, which serves the Yamanote, Yurakucho, Seibu Ikebukuro, Tobu Tojo, Seibu Yurakucho and Marunouchi Lines. Ikebukuro Station is the second busiest train station in the world, surpassed only by its neighbor, Shinjuku Station, which serves the Yamanote, Keio, Shinjuku, Oedo, and Odakyu Lines. So, as I traveled to and from the conversation school in Shinjuku where I worked, I navigated the world's two busiest train stations…twice each day.

In the beginning however, both coming and going, I was utterly lost. None of the streets had names, and both of the train stations had dozens of unmarked exits and tiled access tunnels, all of which looked exactly alike to me. What's worse, it was early March and still freezing cold most of the time, so each evening, when I finally emerged at ground level from some nameless exit and got my bearings, I had no choice but to make my way home along the dark city streets the best way I knew how.

Over time however, the details of my daily commute gradually came into focus and I became quite familiar with the most expeditious route from home to the station, from the station to the school and back again. Eventually, I even refined it to the point of calculating exactly where to stand on the platform to board the train car that would land me nearest my exit.

But the moment of truth came one Friday afternoon as I was on my way out to Toshimaen, where I taught English lessons on my day off to several groups of school-age students at our landlady's little cram school. The suburb of Toshimaen is a good ways out of town, and to get there, I had to ride the Seibu-Ikebukuro Line for about 20 minutes each way. It was my habit to buy a newspaper at one of the station kiosks to pass the time on the train. But on this particular day, an eye-catching headline captured my immediate attention, and I couldn't wait until I had boarded the train to read the story. Instead, I opened up the paper, and read it as I walked. About halfway to the terminal I realized that I had gotten so absorbed in my newspaper that I'd lost track of my whereabouts. I stopped and looked around in the midst of all the rush hour commuters hurrying to and fro, and somehow I still knew exactly where I was and how to get where I was going. That's when I knew that if I could navigate my way through Ikebukuro Station with my nose buried in a newspaper, my days of getting lost in the labyrinth of Tokyo's train stations were truly a thing of the past. ❖

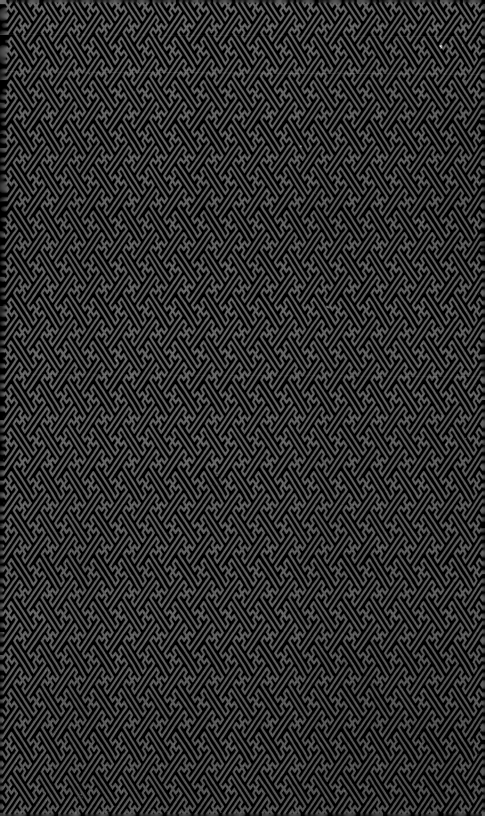

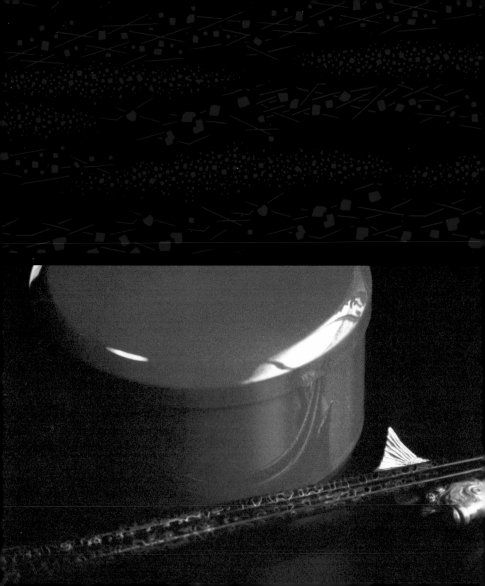

Chopsticks Taboo

What could be more innocuous than a pair of chopsticks? At any given moment, there must be several billion sets of them circulating around Japan. But believe it or not, this seemingly benign and ubiquitous utensil has the power to render its user a social outcast at the merest gaff.

On my first day teaching English, I went across the street to the basement level of My City Department Store during my break and bought some take-out tempura and a scoop of potato salad for my lunch. I returned to the teachers' lounge to enjoy it in the company of my co-workers, and had just dived into the potato salad with a pair of chopsticks when I realized that I had no napkin. Not wanting to lay my chopsticks on the coffee table, I stuck them firmly into the potato salad and set the dish down to go in search of a napkin. At that, I heard a gasp of horror from several of the teachers.

"What?" I inquired naively. "What'd I do?" It seems that I had committed the ultimate breach of etiquette, as I was promptly informed by Judy, a rather intense young Australian woman, that offerings of food with chopsticks standing upright in them are presented to the spirits of the dead at funerals and gravesites, and to do so among the living is strictly taboo. And that's not all. I soon learned that one should never point or otherwise gesticulate with chopsticks, that chopsticks should never be used to spear a morsel of food, and that the end of the chopstick that has been in your mouth should never be used to take food from a shared plate. And as if that weren't enough, food should also never be passed from one set of chopsticks to another because it is reminiscent of a ritual practiced at funerals in which the charred remains of the deceased are transferred from the crematory chamber to the burial urn by passing them from person to person using chopsticks.

So, when it comes to chopsticks, if you want to stay out of trouble, the best rule of thumb is never to let them stray from the short and narrow path between your plate and your mouth. ✤

As *the* Crow Flies

In the world of ornithology, they're known as *Corvus macrorhynchos*. The Japanese call them *hashibuto garasu*. To anyone trying to get a peaceful night's sleep in Tokyo, they're just a plain old nuisance. What I'm talking about, is the common crow. Technically speaking, they're large-billed *jungle* crows, but that doesn't make them any less annoying.

These urban birds roost in the treetops of Tokyo's many public parks and gardens, and at the very first photon of sunlight that shows itself on the horizon each morning, they take to the skies in search of the banquet that has been served up to them on the city streets in clear plastic trash bags. According to bird-watching experts, these flying vermin are so clever that they routinely return to feed at the same spot because they know what delicacies await them there, tearing open the garbage bags because they have come to recognize the shape and color of their favorite tidbits.

This would be fine, (after all, they *are* God's creatures, just like you and me), except that they seem to find it necessary to broadcast their intentions to the entire neighborhood at the first whisper of dawn each morning with a mocking "Haa…haa," as if to say, "Who cares if you're trying to sleep. I'm off to revel in the world's most delicious garbage! Haa…haa."

As a matter of habit and preference, I have never been much of a morning person. Although there have been times throughout my life in which my responsibilities have dictated otherwise, my time in Tokyo was not one of them, since my workday started at the civilized hour of two in the afternoon. Coincidentally, the only English television programming to be had on the Tokyo airwaves was scheduled a couple of nights a week, and didn't begin until two a.m., at which time they featured such cinematic jewels as *Sheena, Queen of the Jungle* and *The Rocky Horror Picture Show*. Fine films indeed, but starved as I was for any form of entertainment in a language I could comprehend, I could never resist the urge to stay up watching, sometimes as late as four a.m. Not to worry though. On movie nights, I could sleep 'til noon, get my eight hours and still make it to work in plenty of time. But the crows…

What's worse, Japan does not observe Daylight Savings Time, and throughout the spring and summer seasons, as the declination of the sun rose higher and higher in its diurnal path, the sunrise came earlier and earlier each day, until the summer solstice, when it began to paint the skies an eerie shade of pink at the merciless hour of 3:30 a.m. On those days, the black devils were at it before I'd even laid my head on my pillow, having their wicked sport with me, reminding me how foolish I'd been to have stayed up so late. "Haa…haa."

Throughout my entire stay in Tokyo, the crows and I never did make our peace with each other. I continued to stay up as late as I pleased, while they continued to mock me at the first flicker of dawn each morning. "Haa…haa." But at least *I* didn't have to eat *garbage* for breakfast. ❖

Takada-san

Ikebukuro Flat, a building that is no longer standing, was a
non-descript, eight-unit apartment house tucked away on a
side street in the third *chome* of West Ikebukuro. Ours was the
first apartment on the ground floor, so I never had reason to
pass by the doors of the other tenants, and thus never made
the acquaintance of any except Takada-san, the man who lived
with his wife and teenaged daughter in the apartment directly
above ours.

From the day that I first met Takada-san, I knew there was
more to him than meets the eye. Over time, I learned that he
and his wife Koko, ran a ballroom dance studio in the Sunshine
60 Building in East Ikebukuro, and had once been champions
in international ballroom dance competitions. In addition to
ballroom dancing, Takada-san had a passion for the game of
mah jongg, and routinely spent his weekend evenings playing
for money in a neighborhood mah jongg parlor. He and Mark
became fast friends, often enjoying the televised *sumo basho*
together on Sunday afternoons and sharing gourmet cooking
secrets afterwards.

Takada-san's apartment was identical to ours, with a large,
combination living room and kitchen, and a smaller *tatami*
room separated by a sliding divider, a fact that would bear little

cause for comment except that Takada-san had, for some unknown reason, shown Mark his bank book, revealing himself to be a veritable millionaire. I would never have guessed by his behavior and lifestyle, and found it rather ironic that he chose to live in such a humble abode.

But again, there was always something understated about Takada-san, as evidenced by the occasion of his first contact with us. One Saturday night, after an evening out at a nearby pub, we invited a friendly couple we'd met there to continue the conversation in our home. As always, our piano was irresistible, and inspired a round of song. We weren't especially rowdy, but the resonance of the piano must have permeated the walls of the building and wafted up through the ceiling to Takada-san's apartment. The following morning, we found a small note taped to our front door. All it said was, "Japan is a small country." ❖

Just a Little Off the Top

The week before I left California for Japan, my stylist gave me a chic but high-maintenance haircut. It was an asymmetrical, upswept do that suited me somehow, but after a couple of untended months in Tokyo, it grew more and more ragged around the edges, until I awoke one Friday morning in obvious need of a trim. That was the day I ventured out for my first and only haircut in Japan.

The decision was so spontaneous that I'd hardly had time to do any research or to ask around for recommendations. I'd noticed a few neighborhood salons on my way to and from work each day, but they all looked a little old-ladyish, and I didn't envision myself walking out of any of them with a hairstyle I'd be pleased or comfortable with. Then it occurred to me that most department stores in cosmopolitan cities have walk-in salons with competent stylists at modest prices, and I reasoned that Japan must have something similar. So I headed *sans appointment* to Seibu Department Store, a glitzy retailer above the west side of Ikebukuro Station. I'd passed it every day on my way to work and knew it to be a first-class establishment.

Just inside the main entrance of Seibu, I checked the store directory and took the escalator up to the salon with my trusty pocket dictionary in hand, thumbing its pages in search of the words "shampoo" and "trim." It was early on a Friday afternoon, yet when I arrived, the waiting room was empty, and it was several minutes before anyone appeared at the reception counter to greet me. As I stood there waiting for someone to acknowledge my presence, I began to doubt whether this was such a good idea after all, and perhaps I should rethink the notion of just trimming it myself. I had almost lost my nerve and decided on the latter, when an apologetic young woman emerged from the inner sanctum of the salon, bowing profusely with an, "*Irashaii mase*," and many a demure, "*Gomen nasai.*"

In my best Japanese, I inquired whether I might have a shampoo and a trim without an appointment. Her response of, "*Hai dozo*," and "*Haite kudasai*," meant that I was in luck, and the young lady ushered me through the curtained doorway into the salon.

The place was immaculate, and it too was empty. It seems that on this particular Friday afternoon, I was the only person in the whole city of Tokyo who wanted a haircut at Seibu Department Store. The young lady seated me at a mirror in the center of the room and disappeared behind yet another curtained doorway to fetch a stylist. A few moments later, not one, but *four* stylists (three young ladies and a young man) filed into the salon and lined up along the wall next to the doorway. I could see them in the mirror as they sized me up from across the room, and I watched with amusement as they engaged in a discreet round of whispered negotiations that probably went something like, "*I'm not gonna do it, you do it…You're the one who speaks English…But I've never cut a foreigner's hair before…I'm not gonna do it…You do it…Besides, you're the senior stylist…I'm not gonna do it. You do it.*"

All at once, the three young ladies nudged the young man reluctantly forward, and he crossed the distance to my chair as if to his doom. After a polite but awkward greeting, I set about the task of communicating how I wanted him to cut my hair. Somehow, with a crude sketch on a small notepad, and the exchange of a few simple words in both Japanese and English, I managed to convey to him that I wanted my complicated hairstyle evened out into a simple, chin-length bob.

Between the consultation and the cut, I was treated to a luxurious, triple shampoo, followed by a rich, fragrant conditioner; and for the finale: an elaborate and invigorating scalp massage. When I returned to my chair, the stylist awaited, scrubbed and smocked, his scissors poised to begin.

With great trepidation, and the precision of a neurosurgeon, he proceeded to nip impossibly tiny bits from the end of each hair, pausing every few minutes to show me his progress in a hand mirror. His co-workers had gathered behind him, close at hand to offer advice and support. He consulted with them frequently throughout the process, and although I was charmed at the meticulous dedication with which he approached his craft, I was also concerned that, in order to make it to my afternoon classes on time, I might have to leave the place with half a haircut. After a while however, once he'd relaxed and regained his confidence, I could see my chin-length bob taking shape. Finally, an hour and a half later, much to the relief of all involved, I walked out of Seibu Department Store with *t-h-e* perfect haircut. ❖

Love Hotel

Kicking around the city of Tokyo and checking out various neighborhoods was my favorite way to spend Sunday afternoons. One sunny Sunday, I decided to explore my own neighborhood instead, and headed over to Higashi Ikebukuro, just across the tracks of the Yamanote Line from where I lived. I was on my way to the Sunshine 60 Building, which at that time was the tallest skyscraper in Asia, and along the way, I passed a Baskin & Robbins ice cream parlor. It was a warm day, and the temptation was just too great to resist, so I ordered myself a scoop of butter pecan and went back outside to enjoy it in the sunshine.

I'd also heard that this particular part of town was known for a stretch of love hotels, and I soon discovered that from the plaza where I sat eating my ice cream cone, I was looking right at it. Even if you've never been to one, the term "love hotel," or *rabu hoteru* as the Japanese call them, is self-explanatory. The rooms in these establishments rent by the hour, and often feature fantasy-theme décor. Love hotels have names like *Dreamland* and *Yes Yes*, and the parking garages are discreetly hidden from view by drive-through curtains. One can well imagine a love hotel as the site of many an infidelity, but in Japan, where single adults often still live with their parents, it's the perfect place to consummate young love.

People-watching has always been one of my favorite pastimes, and Tokyo is an excellent venue for it. On this particular day, I spotted an attractive young Japanese couple standing on the sidewalk outside one of the aforementioned love hotels. They seemed to be deliberating or negotiating over what I could only guess was whether or not to go in and get a room. This went on for several minutes, with the young man tugging gently at the young lady, doing his best to persuade her. The young lady, all the while, was coyly resisting. Finally, the young man won her over and they quickly ducked into the entrance. For the next few seconds, with my eyes still fixed on the spot where they'd stood, I sat smiling at the scene I'd just witnessed, when all of a sudden, out they came again. The young man shook his head, threw up his hands, and turned on his heel, with the young lady pleading sheepishly after him. After a few steps, he put his arm lovingly around her shoulder, she buried her face in his jacket, and off they went. ❖

Be It Ever So Humble

The welfare system in Japan is what one might call "cradle-to-grave." With its highly socialized infrastructure of government ministries, educational institutions, and health care providers, amid a cultural ideology based on the concept of the extended family, even the lowliest of Japan's citizens have ample access to the basic amenities of life. The literacy, longevity, and per capita income rates in Japan are among the highest in the world; and the unemployment, homelessness, and infant mortality rates are among the lowest. Nevertheless, there are still those who manage to slip through the cracks.

They can be seen here and there throughout the city, camped out under railway bridges, huddled in public parks next to open fires, and on rare occasions, wandering dazed and ragged on the city sidewalks of downtown Tokyo. These individuals are not given to panhandling or otherwise harassing pedestrians. Instead, they keep to themselves, or congregate in small circles, engaging in camaraderie and commiseration. During the rainy season, and the cold winter months, the train stations provide an alternative form of refuge for the homeless. And although there is probably an ordinance against loitering and sleeping in the train terminals, the station patrolmen do not appear to enforce it.

During my time in Japan, I took notice of one particular fellow whom I passed each morning and evening near the main entrance of Ikebukuro Station. He was squat and sturdy of build, with broad facial features behind an unkempt mop of jet-black hair, and his skin was dark and leathery from years of exposure to the elements. His habitat consisted of nothing more than a flattened cardboard carton and a small radio. I often wondered how he kept it supplied with batteries. In the early afternoons when I passed by, he was usually still asleep, seemingly oblivious to the trample of feet that passed within inches of his head. When I returned from work in the evenings, I would find him awake and alert, chatting with others of his kind, often enjoying a can of beer or sake from one of the station's vending machines. But no matter what time of day I passed by, he was always clean and always dignified, as he sat on his cardboard mat, with his shoes set neatly to the side. ❖

Yakimo

In cities and villages throughout Japan, street vendors peddle a tempting array of foods, from roasted chestnuts to steaming bowls of noodles. One rustic favorite, a kind of yam, which the Japanese call *yakimo*, can be found roasting in neighborhood markets around suppertime in makeshift braziers made from fifty-five gallon drums. And although the skins of the yams give off a distinctively acrid aroma as they scorch over the coals, the roasted flesh of the potato within is golden and savory.

Some enterprising vendors convert their braziers into rolling carts and take to the streets to peddle their fare. *Yakimo* vendors amble along the narrow passageways between the rows of houses, filling the air with the pungent aroma of the scorching skins, and the simple melody of their song, which consists of six plaintive notes that some strolling vendors sing endlessly into the wee small hours of the morning. *Ya–KI–mohhhh, YAHHHH–ki–mohhhh.*

One evening, on my way home from the station after a late evening out with friends, I walked past the familiar drive-through curtains that concealed the parking garage of a love hotel in my neighborhood. There were no lights in the windows, and no sign of anyone stirring within. Yet the yakimo vendor was still out and about, and even before he rounded the corner, I recognized the familiar fragrance of the roasted yams and the sound of the *Yakimo* Song wafting through narrow streets. *Ya–KI–mohhhh, YAHHHH–ki–mohhhh.* I nodded at him and walked on, wondering how often, if ever, two lovers with a sudden craving after a night of impassioned infidelities, leaned out of the window of the love hotel and called out for *yakimo*. ❖

Goin' Home

The city of Tokyo is mostly steel and concrete. It is so crowded that every millimeter of space is utilized to its fullest capacity, with very little wasted on aesthetics or landscaping. Residential homes and apartments in the inner city do not typically have yards or gardens, and those that do are concealed from view with concrete walls. This Bauhaus approach to civil engineering would be understandably depressing, if not for the hundreds of public parks and temple gardens that provide a welcome respite from Tokyo's urban blight.

In addition to the sprawling acreage of parks such as Yoyogi Koen, Hibiya Koen, Shinjuku Gyoen, Ueno Koen, and Korakuen, every neighborhood has its own little postage-stamp-sized park or garden, with swings for the children and perhaps a horseshoe pit or a shuffleboard court for the elders. On any given street in the residential areas, one might also happen upon a tiny neighborhood temple, with its own quiet little garden where anyone can sit and enjoy a few moments of peace and solitude. Establishments known as "wedding hotels" have the most opulent gardens of all, and their proprietors don't seem to mind if outsiders pay a discreet visit.

But no matter what kind of garden, or its location, all are meticulously maintained and feature the requisite topiary

sculptures, koi ponds, arched bridges and stone lanterns. A walk in a Japanese garden is an elegant and relaxing way to spend a Sunday afternoon.

Most parks and gardens close at six p.m., and the groundskeepers have a uniquely charming way of letting visitors know that it's time to go. At about five minutes to six every evening, the speaker systems in the parks broadcast the dulcet melody of the *Largo* from Antonin Dvorak's *Symphony #9: From the New World.*

The Bohemian composer wrote the New World Symphony while on a visit to Spillville, Iowa, and in it he incorporated the familiar musical themes of traditional Negro spirituals. One called *Massa Dear* inspired the famous English-horn melody of the *Largo*, played at closing time in parks all over Japan. A few years later, William Arms Fisher, one of Dvorak's students turned the melody into a neo-spiritual, the lyrics of which are, "Goin' home, Goin' home, I am goin' home." ❖

Forbidden Fruit

When it comes to the growing scarcity of Mother Nature's resources, the Japanese viewpoint differs significantly from the contemporary Western indoctrination. With the intense media focus on endangered species and the shrinking rain forests, Americans, as a whole, have become increasingly more eco-conscious. We recycle our garbage, we carpool to work, we buy "eco-friendly" products at the grocery store, we vilify furriers, and we donate our hard-earned dollars to such causes as Greenpeace and the National Wildlife Federation. Not that Japan doesn't have its share of eco-conscious citizens, mind you, but the prevailing ideology is quite different from that of the average American.

As a rule, I try to refrain from making blanket generalizations and stereotypical assumptions about individuals of any given race or culture. But having spent well over 10,000 hours talking to the Japanese people for a living, I'd like to think that I have a pretty good grasp of the status quo. When it comes to natural resources, as best I can tell, the Japanese believe that all earth's bounty was put here for human use and consumption, and as long as those resources are utilized for a noble and necessary purpose, with as little waste as possible, then it's all fair game.

Just around the corner from where I lived in Tokyo, there was (and still is) a little neighborhood restaurant called *Ganbi*. Its name is derived from the laurel tree, and the proprietor is a gentle fellow, known to all as Ka-chan. And while the décor of *Ganbi* leaves much to be desired, Ka-chan is arguably one of the best chefs in all of Japan. What I wouldn't give right now for a taste of his tempura.

One Friday evening, upon returning from my lessons in Toshimaen, I stopped at *Ganbi* for a bite to eat at the counter, where I was sure to enjoy a bit of light conversation as well. By now, I had become a familiar face at *Ganbi*, and all the regulars knew who I was. Sitting next to me at the counter was a fellow named Muraka-san, whom I'd met a couple of times before. While I was deciding what to order, Ka-chan served him a plate of *sashimi*, which is nothing more than several perfect slices of raw fish, garnished with a little grated *daikon* radish. However, this particular plate of sashimi was darker than any I'd seen. In fact, it was so blood-red that I thought for a moment it might be raw beef instead.

"*Sorewa nan desuka*," I asked, inquiring the name of the dish in front of him. "*Kujira desu*," he replied. Of course I'd learned early on in Japan never to go anywhere without my pocket dictionary, which was already on the counter, poised to serve me in the event that any unfamiliar words came up in conversation. I thumbed its pages until I found the entry for *kujira*, while the other patrons watched with amusement as my facial expression turned to horror. It seems that my friend Muraka-san was enjoying a few choice morsels of whale! "*Hai dozo, tabate kudasai*," he said, offering me his plate.

Now, I've always fancied myself to be pretty open-minded and adventurous when it comes to food. In addition to untold quantities of sushi, I've eaten goat, rabbit, squirrel, venison, snails, squid, and even alligator. But despite the insistent goading and jeering of the other diners at the counter, that evening in *Ganbi*, whether out of genuine concern for the species, a feeling of abject guilt, or plain and simple brainwashing, I could not bring myself to allow a single bite of whale to pass my lips. ❖

Geisha with a Mohawk

On any given day, you never know who you're going to see when you're out and about in Tokyo. On a rainy weekday, it might be a group of Japanese kindergarten children on their way to an educational event, all wearing bright yellow rain slickers. On a Sunday afternoon in the off season, it might be a couple of gargantuan Sumo wrestlers dressed in their blue and white *yukata*, and wooden *geta*, heading back to the stable after a day in downtown Shinjuku. You might catch a glimpse of a Buddhist monk, head bowed under his straw lampshade of a hat, or a company baseball team in matching uniforms on their way to engage in the harmony of spirit known as *wa*.

The traditional Japanese lifestyle is a serene and conservative one, in which conformity and group mentality are key. At opposite ends of the contemporary spectrum, some individuals still live within the bounds of the strictest of classical tradition and dress accordingly, while many members of the younger generation strive to declare their independence with a bold fashion statement. Most of the population falls somewhere in between, dressing stylishly yet conservatively in western-style clothing. Still, the extremes are there to be observed on occasion.

One day, while riding the Yamanote, I was struck by the beauty of a Japanese woman in full *kimono*: One of deep blue floral silk, bound at the midriff by a bright orange *obi*. Her hair was meticulously coifed, her face was powdered to perfection with pure white rice dust, and her lips were painted with brilliant red precision. She was stunning, and although I tried not to stare, I couldn't take my eyes off her. She was like a rare and exotic flower, and I could only wonder who she was and where she was going dressed like that.

The seat next to her was empty, and at the next station, a young man boarded the train and sat down beside her. In all my life, I have never seen such a contrast in humanity. The young man was dressed in what the Japanese call *panku stairu*, an expression literally borrowed from the English term "punk style." He was all black leather and chains, from his knee-high boots to his skin-tight pants and open vest; and he wore the requisite studded bands around his neck and wrists. His costume was unoriginal, certainly nothing that I hadn't seen dozens of times in San Francisco's Castro District, except that this young man's crowning glory was a bright orange Mohawk, varnished with hair gel until it stood straight up from his scalp to an altitude of no less than a foot. He was magnificent.

So there they sat, the Geisha and the Punk, side by side on the Yamanote, neither taking any particular notice of each other, but creating a snapshot that will live forever in my mind's eye. ❖

Tsukebe

Alas, not every story about Japan is a pleasant one, but at least this one ends well. On a Sunday evening, while riding a crowded Yamanote train on my way back from a day in Harajuku, I witnessed a middle-aged Japanese businessman fondling the *derriere* of an attractive young woman standing next to him. It's a common occurrence on crowded trains. The men who do it are called *tsukebe*, and, sad but true, the accepted response is for the young woman to endure it in silence, lest she draw the disapproving stares of fellow passengers by making a vociferous protest of any kind.

The two of them stood within inches of me. The young woman, dressed in a short, closely-fitted white linen skirt and a bright pink blouse, blushed with humiliation verging on tears, as the man, who stared vacantly into space, ran his hands up and down her thighs and buttocks. I was mortified for her, but knowing as I did that making a scene would only cause her more shame and embarrassment, I didn't react in the way I would have liked. I had already decided that if it ever happened to me, the man who dared to touch me would rue the day; disapproving stares of my fellow passengers be damned!

Meanwhile, I couldn't just stand by and watch while the *tsukebe* continued to victimize that young woman. So instead of lashing out at him, I took a more subtle approach. The next time the man put his hand on her, I touched her shoulder and asked, "Do you speak English." Instantly the man withdrew his hand and moved aside. I could see the gratitude in her eyes as I continued to engage her in simple conversation. When the train stopped at the next station, the young woman thanked me and got off, not because it was her destination, but more likely to continue her journey home…on another train. ✤

Baka

Throughout most of my time in Japan, I was treated like royalty. Total strangers would stop me on the street just to say hello. The Japanese people showered me with gifts, treated me to dinner in expensive restaurants, and welcomed me into their homes. Needless to say, I was taken aback when anyone was less than cordial to me.

I had been living and working in Tokyo for more than a year the first time it happened. It was a cold, gray day, and I was walking around Shinjuku on my lunch break when I noticed a bit of a tickle in the back of my throat. I still had four more hours of teaching ahead of me and I thought I'd best buy myself some cough lozenges to get me through the rest of my workday. I spotted a sundries kiosk near the station that offered a selection of over-the-counter-remedies, so I picked up a roll of honey-lemon drops and dug into my coin purse for ¥100 to pay for them.

The proprietor of the kiosk was an old Japanese woman, and when I offered to put the coins in her hand, she hissed and swore at me in Japanese, gesturing with a gnarled finger for me to put the money on the counter instead. At first, I wasn't sure what she meant, so once again, I held the money out to her; and again, still swearing at me in a raspy voice, she tapped the counter with her finger. I was astonished. This woman was refusing to take the money from my hand. Had I not been in such urgent need of the lozenges, I might have thrown them on the counter and walked away. But I was running late for my next class, so I humbly counted out the ¥100 onto the counter, took my lozenges and left, with the old woman still swearing at me.

Afterwards, as I replayed the scene in my head, fantasizing over what I wish I'd done, it occurred to me that, although I had learned much of the language, I still didn't know a single swear word in Japanese. Up until that moment, I'd never had any need for one. But that old woman made me angry. I hadn't done anything rude to her; I just wanted some cough drops. And I thought it rather ironic that she hadn't refused my *money*, she had just refused to touch my despicable *gaijin* hand. I didn't have to understand a word of Japanese to know that. She'd made it abundantly clear.

When I got back to the school, I recounted the incident to one of my fellow teachers and asked what the appropriate response would have been. As it turns out, just about the worst insult you can hurl at an old woman is the word *baka*, which means fool, idiot, stupid. But in retrospect, even if I'd had that word in my vocabulary, chances are…I probably wouldn't have used it. ❖

Hai-ya!

Before I went to Japan, I had already assumed that the issue of Pearl Harbor and Hiroshima would be a delicate one, and best avoided under any circumstances. But in reality, once I'd been teaching for a while, on those rare occasions that it came up in conversation, I found my Japanese students, most of whom were too young to remember, remarkably unbiased on the issue. No doubt they all harbored their own private feelings, but if that was the case, the majority did not vocalize them. And those who did were of the opinion that it was a matter best relegated to the past, and that we should all move forward in peace. My sentiments exactly.

However, outside the confines of the conversation school, there were those who still subscribed to the old way of thinking. Invariably, they were elders, some of them veterans or widows, who still remembered the hardships of war. Mostly, it was something I sensed, or saw in their eyes. They were understandably bitter, and I felt compassion for them, for they are truly an endearing people and the idea of whole cities being annihilated is unthinkable.

But the entire time I lived in Japan, I was only confronted once in any hostile way. I was walking through one of the yellow-tiled access tunnels to Ikebukuro station on a chilly winter day, where, as with driving, the convention is to keep

to the left. Anyone who forgets will undoubtedly have to dodge a steady stream of oncoming pedestrians headed in the opposite direction.

Midway through the tunnel, about twenty feet ahead, I was faced with a wiry and weathered old Japanese man accompanied by his nurse. Both were headed straight at me, and neither showed any signs of stepping aside. I double-checked my left-right orientation to be sure that I was following the norm and decided that I would politely divert my path around them when the moment came. Just as I veered to the right to avoid them, the old man leaped in front of me with a startling "Hai-ya!" and blocked my path. I was stunned as he crouched before me, with clenched fists and a menacing look in his eyes. So I stepped to the left, in hopes of going around him on the other side. Again he sprang in front of me with a threatening "Hai-ya!" blocking my path, eyes blazing, arms and fists akimbo. The nurse, meanwhile, stood wide-eyed and mute with dismay.

As a last resort, I put up my hands, palms forward in a gesture of capitulation. With a slight bow, I took two steps backward, made a wide circle to the right and continued on my way. And although I will never know exactly what was going through that old man's mind when we met face to face, mine was a small and willing surrender. ❖

Harajuku

Before I left for Japan, J.E.B. Pickett, a friend who'd been there, told me about Harajuku. But I had to see it with my own eyes to believe it.

Just two stops south of Shinjuku Station on the Yamanote Line, Harajuku was once a quaint little district of Tokyo that had its beginnings during the Tokugawa Shogunate as a nothing more than a postal stop on an otherwise desolate northbound route. Harajuku was later assimilated into the Aoyama district at the end of the 16th century, when Shogun Ieyasu Tokugawa awarded Tadanari Aoyama as much land as his horse could travel in a day. Legend has it that Aoyama flogged his poor horse all the way to Nogizaka, where it collapsed and died.

For the next three hundred years, Harajuku remained nothing more than a residential district, until 1915, when construction began on the Meji Jingu Shrine, an elaborate edifice dedicated to the recently deceased Emperor Meji and his wife. The shrine attracted many visitors and the district of Harajuku began to grow in prestige. Sadly, the bombing of Tokyo during World War II left Harajuku and its Meiji Shrine in ruins, and during the U.S. occupation of Japan, a colony of military barracks known as Washington Heights was built in nearby Yoyogi Park.

Over the next two decades however, Harajuku and the Meiji Shrine were restored, but Harajuku as we know it today sprang from the preparations for the 1964 Olympics. The barracks that had once been Washington Heights were converted into dormitories for the Olympic athletes. The requisite Olympic village and two Olympic stadiums were built, and the pathway leading to the Meiji Shrine was transformed into the fashionable, tree-lined boulevard known as Omotesando.

Predictably, both during the Olympics and ever since, the people of Tokyo, especially the younger generation, flocked to Harajuku. NHK's new broadcasting facility in Yoyogi Park added to its appeal, and before long, savvy retailers saw an opportunity to cash in on the market by opening a stretch of trendy boutiques on Takeshita-dori that cater to the steady parade of fashion-conscious teenagers.

To be a teenager in Japan means eight hour school days, followed by four hours of juku study, and mountains of homework, six days a week, ten months a year. So when Sunday comes, they're ready to escape the tedium of their grueling academic curriculum and head for Harajuku for the latest in fashion and music. The day I chose for my first visit was a Sunday as well, and as the train pulled into Harajuku Station, I finally witnessed for myself, the phenomenon my friend J.E.B. had described.

Harajuku Station is built at the top of a small incline, and Takeshita-dori runs perpendicular to it, beginning on its slopes and dipping steeply in the first block. The station affords debarking passengers a bird's-eye view of the boulevard, and when I first saw it, I thought I was hallucinating.

The pavement seemed to be pulsating and undulating. I rubbed my eyes and looked again, only to discover that what I thought was the pavement, was actually a sea of heads: the raven-haired crowns of thousands of teenagers, flowing like the crest of a great river down Takeshita-dori, in search of the latest fashion. ❖

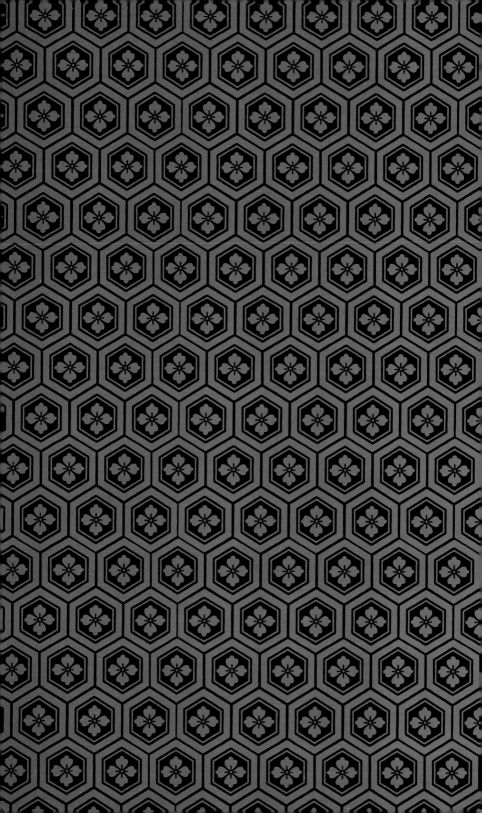

The Legend of Hachiko

One day my friend Kiyoshi called and suggested a rendezvous somewhere in Tokyo. "Where should we meet?" I asked. "How about Hachiko?" he replied. "Where's Hachiko?" I asked. "You don't know Hachiko? It's not a place," he said. "It's a famous statue, near Shibuya Station. Everybody meets there." And so, that's the day I learned the story of Japan's most beloved little dog.

Born in the northern province of Akita, Chu-ken Hachiko, which means "loyal little dog Hachi," arrived in Tokyo in 1924 with his master, Professor Eisaburo Ueno, who had taken a position at the Imperial University. Still just a pup, Hachiko accompanied his master to Shibuya Station each morning, where the professor boarded the train that would take him to the university. Each afternoon at three p.m., Professor Ueno would find Hachiko in the same spot at Shibuya Station, anxiously awaiting his return. Pup and professor continued their daily routine for more than a year, but on May 21, 1925, Hachiko saw his master off at the station for the last time. That fateful day, Professor Ueno suffered a fatal stroke at the university, and never returned home. Nevertheless, Hachiko continued to wait in vain that day, and every day thereafter, for nearly ten years.

Throughout the years, as Hachiko kept his vigil for his beloved master, Professor Ueno's gardener and the Shibuya Station captain fed and cared for him. The story of the loyal little dog spread across Japan, and people began coming from far and wide just to see him and to pat his head for luck. Finally, on March 7, 1934, Hachiko died in the very same spot where he'd spent nearly ten years, patiently waiting for one who never returned.

Word of Hachiko's death made newspaper headlines, and the entire nation mourned the loss of the faithful little dog. Some even sent contributions of money, which were eventually used to commission famed sculptor Teru Ando to create a bronze statue of Hachiko. It was completed in April of 1934, and erected on the very spot where Hachiko perpetually awaited his master.

Alas, during the dark days of World War II, every available scrap of metal, including the beloved bronze statue of Hachiko, was melted down for arms and ammunition, and its sculptor Teru Ando was killed in the war. But in 1948, the Society for Recreating the Hachiko Statue commissioned his son Takeshi Ando to cast a second bronze statue of Hachiko, which stands at the southwest corner of Shibuya Station to this day.

Professor Ueno was buried in Aoyama Cemetery, where another statue of Hachiko continues the vigil for his master at his gravesite. It is even rumored that some of Hachiko's bones are buried there with him. Hachiko himself has been immortalized through the art of taxidermy, and can still be seen, waiting for his master, in the National Museum of Science in Ueno.

When I arrived at Shibuya Station that afternoon, I saw the statue of Hachiko for the first time. It was much smaller than I'd imagined, an unpretentious bronze rendering, and not all that much bigger than life-sized. And as promised, I found my friend Kiyoshi standing next to it, along with hundreds of others, under the vigilant gaze of Hachiko, faithfully waiting for their loved ones to arrive. ❧

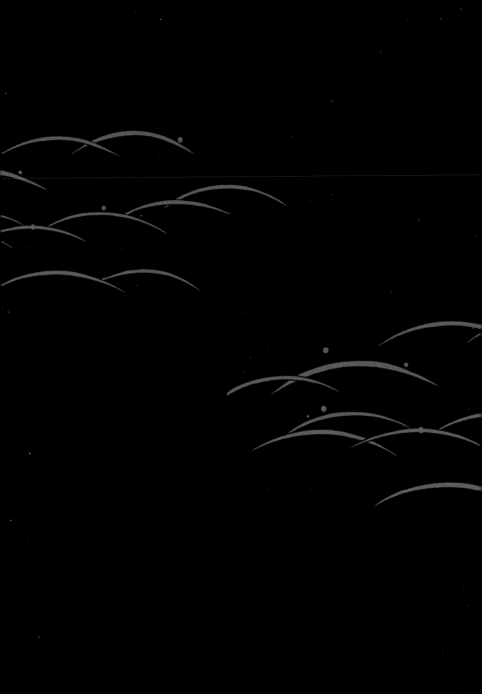

Takao-san

The Japanese use the same honorific for their mountains that they use to show respect for each other. Instead of Mr. or Ms., they add the suffix "–san" to the end of a person's name. In much the same spirit of respect, they also add "–san" to the names of their mountains.

Out in the western suburb of Hachioji, at the very end of the Keio Line, is the mountain known as Takao-san, Tokyo's nearest peak. It rises to a height of almost 2,000 feet and features both a cable lift and a funicular, a counterbalanced incline railway that runs up the side of its eastern slope. The two rail cars are like the weights of a grandfather clock. At both the top and the bottom of the mountain, passengers board the train simultaneously, and the lower car transports passengers to the top, while the upper car returns others to the bottom. The two cars pass each other exactly in the middle.

It's a steep journey to the top, as the pendant train car inches its way up the slopes of Takao-san. Outside the windows, the foliage is lush, and a quaint little station awaits at the top. Beyond the station, several hiking courses wind their way into the crown of the mountaintop. Takao-san was always one of our favorite places to spend a Sunday afternoon, and we visited it frequently during our stay in Japan. On this particular day, we arrived at the top a little later than usual and followed trails and paths on its western slopes that we hadn't explored in previous visits. Toward day's end, we happened upon several small groups of hikers gathered on an unexpected precipice. They appeared to be intently focused on the southwestern sky and, wondering what the attraction was, we turned our gaze in the same direction. Much to our delight, we discovered that we had stumbled upon a perfect view of Fuji-san, the great volcano. Away in the distance, nearly 100 kilometers to the southwest, it hovered on the horizon like a gilded apparition in the golden rays of the autumn sunset.

We were so transfixed by the enchanting vision of Mt. Fuji that we forgot all about the long hike back to the station. And although we ran the entire way, when we arrived, the station was shut tight. The funicular had already made its last descent down the mountain, and there wasn't a living soul to be found. In all the times we'd been there, we'd always made it back in time for the last run of the incline train and had never given a moment's thought to how one might otherwise get down the hill. It had never even occurred to us whether there might be some other way.

But reason prevailed, and a little investigation soon revealed a wide, evenly paved access road that quite obviously led down to the base of the mountain. So in the gloaming twilight of Takao-san, we set off down the path, chatting quietly in the gathering darkness until we reached the bottom of the hill. There we saw the familiar lights of Takaosanguchi Station, where a train on the Keio Line awaited to take us back home to Tokyo. ❖

Takao-san

Hanabi

When translated literally, *hanabi*, the Japanese word for fireworks, means *flower-fire*; and you haven't lived until you've seen fireworks in Japan. On warm evenings throughout the summer season, along the banks of Japan's rivers, the night sky explodes in bursts of fiery color. In fact, these fireworks displays are named for the riverbanks from which they are launched: *Tamagawa Hanabi, Kanagawa Hanabi, Sumidagawa Hanabi*.

By mid afternoon on the day of the fireworks, the rivers are already dotted with sailboats, motorboats and rowboats, all vying for the best location from which to view the spectacle. Rooftops are a popular spot for those lucky spectators with access to a place above the crowd. But mostly, the streets are jam-packed with common folk who have come to enjoy the festivities.

Along its length, as it winds its way through rural Japan and the suburbs of Tokyo, the Sumida River is crossed by many bridges, some of which are quite close together. The Sumidagawa Hanabi are launched over two such bridges, creating a doubly dazzling spectacle. On the day that I was fortunate enough to attend this fireworks display, my companion and I headed for the Sumida River after work, and arrived with little time to spare. Having been offered no invitation to a private rooftop party, we were clueless as to where to view the display, and therefore, had to rely on our intuition. We followed the general migration of the crowd toward what we guessed were the banks of the river. Block by block, as we drew nearer, the crowds became progressively thicker, moving more and more slowly, until we finally reached a standstill, packed like the proverbial sardines, unable to move in any direction.

Ordinarily, I would have worked myself into a state of panic over the closeness of the crowd, but at that moment, there was a deafening boom. The fireworks had begun.

The world around me disappeared as I turned my gaze heavenward. It seems that, as we were propelled along by the crowds, we had somehow magically landed in the epicenter of the event. For the next 90 minutes, we were cascaded with shower after shower of brilliantly sparkling bursts of *flower-fire* on our upturned faces: an experience that defies description with mere words. But imagine, if you will, the biggest, grandest finale of a fireworks show you've ever seen. Multiply that by an hour and a half of non-stop pyrotechnics, and you might come close to picturing the explosive grandeur of the Sumidagawa Hanabi. ❖

The Wolf

I've never been much of a sports fan, and rarely watch any
sporting events except the Kentucky Derby, the World Series,
and the Super Bowl. That's why I thought it more than a little
uncharacteristic of me when I became obsessed…with *sumo*
wrestling. Although I must admit that I found the notion
disgusting at first: All those morbidly obese men, strutting
around nearly naked, engaging in a public spectacle, the object
of which consists of nothing more than trying to shove each
other out of a small circular ring. But after watching my first
sumo basho, while stuck indoors on a rainy Sunday afternoon,
I was hooked.

Before long, I knew the names and ranks of all the wrestlers,
and had chosen my favorites to cheer on. Those were the
heydays of Konishiki, Asahifuji, Akebono, and the legendary
Chiyonofuji, "the Wolf." But as impressive as these grand masters
were, my favorite was a handsome young newcomer and rising
star named Terao. Unlike the most of others, he was fit and
muscular, and although he never did go on to achieve the
same championship and celebrity of the "big four," he was
a spirited young competitor who faced those giants with
courage. I liked his style.

The beauty of sumo is that it's a year-round sport, with
tournaments called *basho* that last for two weeks during

alternate months. There's a *basho* for each season of the year, (*Hatsu, Haru, Natsu*, and *Aki*), and a couple of regional events in between. So, you can get your fill of the sport for a few days, but you don't get too overdosed on it, and you don't have to wait very long for the next one.

I must confess however, that I had little patience for watching sumo in real-time, which can drag on for hours as each pair of wrestlers goes through the salt-throwing ritual, and then they size each other up, circling warily around and around before actually engaging in their all-too-brief battle. Instead, I preferred to watch the ten o'clock rendition, fittingly called *Sumo Digest*. Sumo *Lite*, if you will. This abridged version features only the final few minutes of each match, which showcases the moment of victory, and skips all the formality and fanfare in between.

Chiyonofuji was a sumo wrestler unlike any other. Not only did he capture the hearts of the sumo-watching nation for more than 15 years, moving steadily up the ranks until 1981, when he won two successive tournaments, and rose to the prestigious title of *yokozuna*. He won several championships with perfect 15-0 performances, and accumulated a continuous run of 53 undefeated challenges. Chiyonofuji walked away with 31 championships, and a total of 968 career wins, for which he was awarded the National Medal of Honor.

The requisite hairstyle for sumo wrestlers falls at or below shoulder length. For tournaments, the hair is dressed with oil extracted from the hips of camellia flowers and twisted into a topknot sculpted into the shape of a ginko leaf. When a sumo wrestler retires, the ceremony culminates in the cutting-off of his hair, and one of the most memorable occasions in the history of sumo was the moment that Chiyonofuji, "The Wolf," surrendered his topknot. I watched in tears that day, as Chiyonofuji was shorn like Samson. And although I never enjoyed the privilege of watching him fight in person, I knew that I had witnessed greatness of a kind that the world has never seen before or since. ❖

English à la Carte

To say that the Japanese are naïve in their use of English would be a kindly euphemism, when in fact, what I mean to say is that there were days when I wanted to go out and edit the entire city of Tokyo. In Japan, English in any form is trendy and hip, whether speaking it with foreigners, singing it in *karaoke* bars, or sporting it on some kind of personal accessory. A word or two of it emblazoned on a handbag or a piece of clothing is *tres chic*. Which would be fine, except that its use in Japanese fashion, advertising, and product packaging is often either woefully out of context, or…it's a bunch of incomprehensible gibberish.

Some days I was able to enjoy the humor of it, other days it drove me crazy. I couldn't help but chuckle to myself when I saw something like, "This is boy. Pretty wow guy!" printed on a teenager's knapsack. But there were times when it seemed that everywhere I looked, there was a shopping bag, a product label, a bus placard or a billboard that had shamelessly butchered my mothertongue.

One day the cosmos sent me a little gift that would allow me to transcend the issue once and for all, and never let it bother me again.

It was a workday, and I was on my way out of the building to take my lunch break. The school where I worked was located directly across from the east entrance of Shinjuku Station, above which there are several large department stores, including one called My City, which I could see from the entrance of the building. On this particular afternoon, parked in the loading zone of My City, was a small, white delivery truck, which I guessed must belong to some kind of clothing or accessory designer. The name of the company was printed in stylish lettering on the side of the truck, with the year in which it had been established proudly displayed beneath it. It said:

INFINITY…Since 1987. ❖

The Art of Tea

The tea ceremony is one of Japan's most refined and exquisite traditions. Time stands still in the *tatami* teahouse as the hostess, dressed in her finest silk kimono, meticulously prepares the utensils, patiently waits for the kettle to boil, precisely measures the tea leaves into each bowl, whisks the concoction to foamy perfection, serves it up with the utmost grace in aesthetically appealing porcelain, and watches attentively as her guests partake.

As part of our apartment rental agreement, I taught English lessons every Friday afternoon at the landlady's little after-school *juku* to several groups of Japanese students, ranging in age from pre-school to college. The school was located on the second floor of a utilitarian building in Toshimaen, and admittedly, there were countless other ways in which I'd rather have spent my Fridays off. But the children were so sweet and endearing, and Toshimaen, a quaint neighborhood centered around a tiny amusement park at the end of the Seibu Ikebukuro Line, was a perfectly fine place to spend a couple of hours at week's end.

One day, Mrs. Koyama, the landlady of our apartment and the proprietor of that shabby little school in Toshimaen, announced that a tea ceremony was to be held in lieu of our regular lessons. She provided detailed directions to a modest, yet stunningly beautiful teahouse with a picturesque view of an impeccable Japanese garden. The teahouse had been reserved especially for the occasion, and upon my arrival, I removed my shoes and settled into the traditional kneeling position on the *tatami* floor.

Before the ceremony commenced, I was duly informed of the elements involved in the presentation, and what was expected of the participants. I was instructed to watch the ceremony attentively, to keep my conversation to a polite minimum, and to turn the tea bowl three times to admire its beauty before drinking the tea down in three uniform sips. What I hadn't been told was that this was not just "a" tea ceremony, but rather a series of them, in which five of my students would be demonstrating their achievement in the art of tea.

I was charmed at first to see my favorite students, dressed in kimono, doing their perfect best to demonstrate the tea ceremony for my benefit. But after the second iteration, my knees and ankles began to ache; and by the fourth performance, I was completely numb from the waist down. Moreover, as pure and wholesome as it may sound, a bowl of Japanese green tea contains almost as much caffeine as a cup of coffee. So, after two and a half hours and five bowls of it, when the whole affair was finally over, I was completely wired. And although it took me the rest of the evening and most of the next day to recuperate from its aftereffects, I can honestly say that I have fully experienced the art of tea. ❖

Omikoshi

Amid all its ultra-modern innovations, at its very heart, Japan is still a land of ancient tradition. Each region has its own unique cultural attributes, and most, if not all of their holidays and celebrations are based on some practice that dates back to the earliest days of its civilization. The Japanese celebrate the ephemeral cherry blossoms in spring, they celebrate the vernal and autumnal equinoxes, they celebrate the rice harvest, they celebrate the full moon, they celebrate the Emperor's birthday, and they celebrate the returning spirits of the deceased.

One day, while out and about in the suburb of Ikebukuro, I witnessed one of the liveliest and most dazzling celebrations: the *Omikoshi* parade. It was a beautiful afternoon, and I was headed over to the east side to buy a meter of cloth, when quite unexpectedly, I found myself in the midst of a throng of spectators lining the sidewalk. Over the tops of their heads, I could see an enormous and elaborately embellished structure bobbing along the parade route. It looked something like a miniature temple building, splendidly decorated with Japanese crests and golden filigree. I pushed my way through the crowd for a closer look and discovered that this colossal edifice was actually being heaved along the city streets on the shoulders of about two dozen strapping young Japanese men. What's more, they were dressed in traditional garb, which consists of short, open-front robes called *hanten*, and white cotton loincloths called *mawashi*, leaving their naked chests and buttocks quite exposed.

I was transfixed. I had never seen such an unabashed display of flesh and sinew. All those gorgeous young men, chanting in unison, laboring and sweating in the noonday sun, to transport the statue of their Shinto deity through the streets of Higashi Ikebukuro. It was…spectacular! ❖

Mystery Men

The daily route from my apartment in Ikebukuro to the school where I taught in Shinjuku was quite unremarkable. The walk to the station every day was probably a little under a mile, most of it through small neighborhood streets lined with commonplace homes, ordinary shops and generic office buildings. But after a few months of walking the same path from home to the train station to the school and back again, I came to know every streetlamp and manhole cover. The faces of the neighborhood proprietors grew familiar and each day as I passed them, I would say, "*Ohayo*," to Ohara-san, the lady whose family owned the convenience market, and to the butcher on the corner whose name I never learned, and to Ka-chan, the chef of the little neighborhood restaurant called *Ganbe*.

There was one place in particular, however, that remained a mystery. It was a building in the middle of the block, the entrance of which was always secured by a heavy, gray roll-down door. In all the times I'd passed by, it was never open and there was never a soul to be seen. So imagine my surprise one Saturday evening when I rounded the corner to find that the mystery door had been lifted and there was a party going on inside. Not just an ordinary party, mind you, but a decidedly Japanese, male-only, sake-drinking party.

The interior of the building was one big, empty *tatami* room that had been decorated for the occasion with floral wreaths, and colorful paper lanterns and streamers. About two dozen old men, dressed in traditional Japanese robes, were sitting around on cushions talking and singing and drinking; and although it was raining buckets outside, I couldn't help but stop to stare at them. As I stood there under my umbrella, feet soaking in puddles of rain, wondering what the cause for celebration was, one of the old men gestured for me to come inside and join them. I was overcome with curiosity, and it certainly looked like a lot more fun than trudging back home to an empty apartment, so I did.

I closed my umbrella, took off my shoes and sat down on the *tatami* floor. The old man who had invited me in grinned at me and filled my cup with hot sake. I soon discovered that nobody in the entire group spoke a word of English, so I fished my pocket dictionary out of my bag and made an attempt to communicate with them in Japanese. By this time, I'd been in Japan long enough to have mastered the basics of the language and could carry on simple conversations, although I never did become fluent enough to say anything intelligent or profound.

For the next couple of hours, I enjoyed the revelry and hospitality of those old men, and managed to convey to them that I was an English teacher from California. They all seemed rather

impressed with that, and I became the subject of much head nodding and many an "*Asoka.*" and a "*Honto ni.*" But try as I might, I never learned who those old men were and what they were celebrating. I still wonder to this day. ❖

Round the Clock

English teachers work pretty hard in Japan. Some of them also party just as hard, and there's a *gaijin* bar in West Ikebukuro called One Lucky that caters to the all-night crowd. Although I am given to staying up late, I was never one for staying out partying 'til sunrise and usually began to wane long before my English-teaching compatriots were ready to call it a night. On one particular Saturday night that gradually evolved into a Sunday morning, Mark stayed out drinking and socializing with his chums at One Lucky until it closed at nearly sun-up. I was at home, already in bed, scantily dressed and sound asleep, when I was roused by a fellow named John, a One Lucky regular who had become somewhat of a familiar friend. It took me a couple of minutes in my dream-laden state to comprehend that John had had the courtesy to hurry ahead and warn me that Mark was on his way with a rowdy crowd of people who, upon being turned out by the proprietor of One Lucky, were about to invade my household.

Within a matter of minutes, the living room was full of strangers, most of them drunk. Having just been awakened from my dreams, I was in no mood to party at that hour, and not knowing what else to do, I dragged my futon into the other room, closed the sliding divider and tried to salvage what was left of a night's sleep.

But to my misfortune, there is nothing more enticing to a group of happy drunks than round of song. The prophesied piano that I'd first seen in my dreams now kept me from them, and my unexpected guests indulged in every cliché melody from *Lean on Me* to *House of the Rising Sun*. Finally, at around seven in the morning, I realized that any hopes of getting back to sleep were futile, so I got up, got dressed, slid open the room divider and, on my way out the door, I glowered at the raucous rabble who had now begun to pass out on my living room floor.

Being out and about on the streets of Tokyo at that hour was a new experience for me and I didn't know quite what to do with myself on such an early Sunday morning. So, I bought a newspaper and went first to *Ma-ku-do-na-ru-do*, otherwise known as McDonald's, for an Egg McMuffin and a cup of coffee. When I'd finished my paper and my breakfast, I went for a ride around the Yamanote Line that encircles the city of Tokyo. All 29 stops. The city was beautiful in the morning light, and because always I worked in the afternoons, I'd never seen it at that hour. It was a unique experience.

But when I arrived back at Ikebukuro Station after only an hour, I knew that all those people would still be there in my living room, so I had to find someplace else to go. I don't know what inspired me that day, but the destination I chose to while away a Sunday morning was the Ueno Zoo, and I was waiting outside the gates when it opened at 9:00 a.m.

I'd never been to the Ueno zoo before, nor had I ever been to any zoo when it first opened in the morning. All the animals were on their best behavior, and just inside the entrance, in one of the first exhibits, a peacock fanned its tail for me. It was stunning in the morning sunlight, and in that moment, all was forgiven: The rowdy camaraderie of strangers in my living room, the rousting from my bed at seven a.m. on a Sunday morning, and the chore of finding a way to kill time until they all woke up with their hangovers and went home.

With the exception of John, I never bothered to get to know any of the people in my living room that morning. I was too mad at them. And yet I am grateful to each and every one of them for rousing me from my sleep, for giving me a reason to visit the Ueno Zoo, and especially for propelling me to ride the Yamanote all the way around on a beautiful Sunday morning for the first and only time. ❖

Kimono

The English conversation school where I worked had a policy
against teachers fraternizing with students. That's why I was a
little apprehensive when Junko Watarai, a young lady who was
practiced in the traditional arts of the tea ceremony, flower
arranging and kimono dressing, asked if we could meet outside
of class sometime. But because she was tempting me with the
rare opportunity play dress-up in her kimono, I was willing
to risk a reprimand, and discreetly gave her directions to
my apartment.

It was a sweltering Sunday afternoon when Junko arrived with
a large, well-worn but elaborately embellished pasteboard box,
the kind that department stores use to wrap expensive clothing.
We sequestered ourselves in the *tatami* room with a couple of
cold sodas, where Junko revealed the complex trappings secreted
within the box and proceeded to work her magic.

The most important element of wrapping a kimono is to create
a smooth line, and although I've never thought of myself as
buxom, Junko's first task was to bind my breasts flat. Next she
placed a small, rolled towel around my collarbone to create a
clean vertical line from neck to hips. A light muslin slip formed
the next layer, to keep the kimono from making direct contact
with my perspiring skin.

Once I was trussed and muslin-ed, Junko slipped a gorgeous, blue–floral kimono on my shoulders and arranged the front, left over right. On any other day, I might have luxuriated in its delicate brocade weave and silken texture, but the temperature and the humidity were both well above ninety, and I was nearly ready to faint when Junko began tying the *obi*. The sash was a dazzling shade of chartreuse green, garnished with a tasseled orange cord, and after wrapping it snugly around my midriff, she tied the cumbersome ends into an elaborate bow in the back, a technique that is traditionally reserved for young, unmarried women.

As if icing on the cake, Junko applied make-up to my face and styled my hair, and afterwards she took photos. And although, when all was said and done, I was still just a *gaijin* in a kimono on a miserably hot day, I must admit that being fussed over all afternoon and dressed in kimono right-by-the-book made me feel quite special; and the photos of me wearing it are among the most treasured in my collection. ❖

Shichi-Go-San

All children are beautiful, and Japanese children are among the most adorable in the world. Their parents treat them like gold, and even have a special day called *Shichi-Go-San*, which means Seven-Five-Three, to honor children of these ages. *Shichi-Go-San* is held on November 15, a time of year when the days are cool, clear, and golden with the autumn foliage. And although celebrations are held at shrines all over Japan, on this day, the place to see and be seen is Meiji Jingu in Shibuya.

The enormous shrine, built to honor the Emperor Meiji and his wife, is the location of choice for parents to bring their children to give thanks for their good fortune, to pray for their children's health and longevity, and to be blessed by a Shinto priest. According to history and tradition, in *samurai* times, at age three, both boys and girls, who typically had shaven heads, were allowed to grow their hair. At age five, boys were allowed to wear *hakama* trousers, and at age seven, girls were allowed to wear *obi* sashes instead of cords to tie their kimono. Based on these rites of passage in a child's life, boys and girls aged three, boys aged five, and girls aged seven participate in the *Shichi-Go-San* ceremonies.

Children come to Meiji Jingu dressed in their very finest garments: colorful kimono with obi sashes for the girls, and *haori* robes and *hakama* trousers for the boys. They line up, sometimes for hours, to await their turn with the presiding priest. Once inside the main hall of the shrine, the priest recites an individual prayer for a long, healthy, prosperous life for each child. After the blessing, the child is presented with a gift of long sticks of candy called *chitose-ame*, which means "thousand year sweets." The candy comes wrapped in ornate bags decorated with cranes and turtles, both symbols of longevity.

I couldn't have asked for a more perfect day on the occasion that I had the good fortune to attend *Shichi-Go-San* at Meiji Jingu. The children were there in abundance, each one more adorable than the last, and although I hadn't included motherhood in my Japan itinerary, unbeknownst to me on that lovely afternoon, according to my calculations, I was already with child. ❖

Mt. Fuji

Of all the symbols and icons that represent Japan, Mount Fuji is by far, the most inspiring and powerful. Located inland about forty-five miles southwest of Tokyo, it rises with near-perfect symmetry above the landscape to a height of twelve thousand three hundred eighty-five feet. The great volcano hasn't erupted since 1707, yet wisps of steam can still be seen rising hundreds of feet into the air. Some believe that the sleeping giant will awaken again someday.

Fuji has many faces. For much of the year, it remains hidden by a veil of clouds. On clear days in the spring, capped with a mantle of pure white snow, its slopes appear deep blue in the distance. Up close, the surface is an ashen and forbidding rubble of once-molten rock. On a relief map of Japan, Mt. Fuji looks like a violent blow-out in the surface of the earth. And although it can be seen from Tokyo, and just about everywhere else in the central region of Honshu, it was several months before I finally saw Mt. Fuji with my own eyes.

It was on a day in early October that I caught my first glimpse of it. The weather was overcast on the trip to Kyoto, and the leaden skies shrouded much of the landscape. I was following the map and watching expectantly as the countryside whizzed by at 150 miles an hour, when all at once, I spotted the familiar silhouette on the horizon. But in less time than it took to say, "Here comes Mt. Fuji…That's Mt. Fuji…There goes Mt. Fuji," it was all over. The train was traveling so fast that, had I blinked, I might have missed it altogether, and the sullen peak in no way resembled any photograph I'd ever seen of it. I was crestfallen.

However, over the next two years, Fuji revealed and redeemed itself a dozen times over as it appeared out of nowhere at the most unexpected times and places. On a visit to the town of Kofu in Yamanashi Prefecture in which I had arrived after dark, I awoke the next morning to find Mt. Fuji in all its glory right outside my bedroom window. On a hike up Mt. Takao on the western outskirts of Tokyo, just at sunset, Fuji appeared as a golden apparition on the horizon. One Sunday afternoon in downtown Shinjuku, from the observation deck on 51st floor of the Sumitomo Building, Fuji revealed itself yet again, like a tiny treasure glimmering in the distance. And on that cold day in February when at last I bade a reluctant farewell to Japan, outside the window of the plane, on the horizon just beyond the tarmac, her parting gift…a perfect view of Mt. Fuji. ❖

Ryoanji

Although I am not a practitioner of Zen Buddhism, I have always been drawn to its ideology and try to incorporate its precepts into my daily life. So when the chance presented itself for a visit to Ryoanji, Japan's most famous Zen garden, I was ecstatic. For me, it was tantamount to a visit to Mecca or the Vatican.

The name Ryoanji means Temple of the Peaceful Dragon, and the original site of Ryoanji Temple is over a thousand years old; having been awarded by the Tokudaiji family to the warlord Katsumoto Hosokawa, who established a temple on the grounds in the year 983. The garden itself was added during a restoration of the site in 1488 and is a mere five hundred years old. It measures thirty meters long by ten meters wide and is comprised of fifteen natural stones of various sizes placed on a bed of pure white gravel, raked into meticulous patterns around the stones. The garden is located on the south side of Ryoanji Temple, with a viewing pavilion for visitors on its northern perimeter. A low, earthen wall surrounds the remaining three sides of the garden, with cedar, pine and cherry trees beyond.

Ryoanji is a magnet for tourists year-round, and the day I visited was no different. There were already hundreds of people on the premises when we arrived, many of whom were seated on the viewing pavilion. Nevertheless, I found myself an empty spot and sat down to ponder the mystery of the garden. I'd read a few things in advance about Ryoanji, most notably that from any point in the garden it is impossible to view all fifteen stones at once. One of them always remains hidden from view. They say that the fifteenth stone can only be seen in the mind's eye when spiritual enlightenment has been attained. It is also said that by staring at the stains on the weathered earthen wall, one might experience mystical visions.

As I sat on the viewing pavilion with great expectations, my first feeling was something akin to *The Emperor's New Clothes*. I imagined that everyone else was seeing or experiencing something that I did not. So there I sat, hoping for some kind of small *satori* as I gazed at the hypnotic patterns of the gravel, raked in long, straight rows that, when met with the stones, perfectly encircle them.

I was more than a little surprised and disturbed when the next feeling I experienced was an overwhelming urge to run wildly into the garden and wreak havoc on its austere perfection. I contemplated for the next few moments upon the consequences of such lunacy and prayed for a distraction that would curb my impulses. As an antidote to my unbridled thoughts of vandalizing the sacred garden, I began to count the stones. Almost like a three dimensional haiku, they are arranged in groups of five, two, three, two and three, and I soon discovered that what I'd heard was true: all I could see from my place on the pavilion were fourteen. Which set me to wondering where the fifteenth stone was hidden.

I occupied my mind with that conundrum for the next few minutes, and being unable to solve it without getting up and wandering around, obstructing the view of the other visitors,

I turned my attention to the wall. It had once been painted pure white, but over the years, its surface has been yellowed and weathered by exposure to the elements; and pigmentation from the composition of the natural materials beneath the paint has been leached to the surface by moisture. The effect is a group of sepia-toned images that resemble an ancient parchment map or an ethereal watercolor. I searched those images for a glimpse of the fabled visions, and although I am given to prophetic dreams from time to time, Ryoanji offered none that day.

So that was it. I'd exhausted every avenue of contemplation Ryoanji had to offer and had found nothing. No enlightenment, no transcendence, not even a small *satori*. But just as I was about to rise and walk away, it happened. Sitting on the steps of the viewing pavilion, I came to the realization that there was nothing in the garden. Never was. Never would be. I would only find there what I had brought with me. And when I asked myself what that was, I saw the culmination of my life: All my joy, all my pain, all my accomplishments, all my disappointments, all my fears, and all my dreams. In that moment, something changed. A wave of peace and fulfillment washed over me. All is as it is. The garden of Ryoanji was perfectly empty and still. Like a Zen meditation. And when I looked again, I saw everything…and nothing. ❖

The Fox and the Foreigner

What is life but a series of experiences? And in Japan, even seemingly ordinary days rarely fail to yield some unexpected highlight. But, as with any culture, travel often affords the most memorable ones.

Having spent the better part of a year slaving away in the *Modal Auxiliary Mines* (my term of endearment for the English conversation school in Tokyo where I taught), my companion and I decided to make a long-awaited journey to Kyoto. As promised, the fall season showed itself radiantly, and perhaps nowhere quite as strikingly as in the mystical setting of the ancient capital.

The days were clear and polished, with enormous banks of snow-white cumulus clouds hovering on the horizon's blue-purple hills. At day's end, in the long rays of the October sun, these could banks were transformed into glorious kaleidoscopes of color, soon to be subdued and soothed by the onset of twilight, sparked by the twinkle of the evening star.

Kyoto enchanted us. Kyomizu Temple, with its three fountains for health, wealth, and wisdom, refreshed us. Kinkaku-ji, the temple of gold, both resplendently opulent and ironically unpretentious, dazzled us. Ryoan-ji, the raked sand and pebble garden with its fifteen stones, hypnotized and quieted us.

Outside Kyoto, to the north, the tiny hamlet of Ohara was a two-day haven. Wooded paths, lined with *tatami* tea rooms and local crafts shops, wound their way along the river into the hillsides, which revealed quietly secluded cloisters: Jakko-in, older almost than time itself; Hosen-in, with its garden so meticulously beautiful that the viewer is an essential dimension of its very existence, and Sanzen-in, where barefoot priests entreat visitors to sit for a few quiet moments in contemplative solitude to copy a Buddhist devotional onto fine rice paper with bamboo brushes.

With all of that beauty etched in our memories, we made our way to Nara, another of Kyoto's satellite cities. The day was a national holiday and, predictably, natives and tourists alike made their pilgrimages in tens of thousands.

We soon grew weary of the slow parade and gravitated toward the hills in search of less populated surroundings. Our chosen path led us through a somewhat residential area, and along the way we happened upon a small, sloped pasture where several deer grazed quietly. They were quite tame and I regretted having nothing to feed them. My resourceful companion spotted a persimmon tree laden with fruit, so we picked all that we could reach and fed them to the grateful deer who had long since devoured all of them that *they* could reach.

By now it was past noon, and after the climb into the hills, we were feeling the need for our own repast. The neighborhood offered two choices: a Chinese-style café and a tiny soba restaurant. We opted for the latter because it had a lovely shaded arbor with low benches and a Siamese cat roaming playfully about.

Soba, thin buckwheat noodles served in a savory broth with various toppings, is one of Japan's more palatable dishes. But this particular soba shop, being the out-of-the-way place that it was, provided neither English menus nor English speakers. Armed with my trusty pocket dictionary and knowledge of *katakana* and *hiragana* (the two simplest of Japan's three alphabets) I attempted to decipher the row of wooden paddles on the wall which listed the menu selections. Unfortunately, they were mostly in *kanji* (the third and more difficult pictograph alphabet). And although the waitress kindly pronounced the kanji for us, most of the words were not contained in my now hopelessly inadequate dictionary. Of the entire array, there were only three that I could positively identify: herring, which I detest; egg, which I'm allergic to; and something called KITSUNE (pronounced Keet-soo-nay). Kitsune...Kitsune...I thumbed my dictionary. It was in there alright, it's the Japanese word for FOX! Ye Gods! I thought. If Kitsune is fox, what could all those other dishes possibly be? Possum? Raccoon? My mind ran rampant while my appetite grew more ravenous with each passing moment. And of course my friend, who will eat most anything, ordered the herring soba and left me in a quandary.

It was a long way to the bottom of the hill in search of an alternative lunch, and besides, I was being silly. I should just *order* something. As Kiyoshi, a Japanese friend of mine, is fond of saying whenever I inquire as to the nature of unfamiliar dishes, "It's *food*! Eat it!"

By this time, the restaurant had filled up and suddenly, all around me, I heard requests and orders for "Kitsune soba", "Kitsune soba, futatsu kudasai." ("for two, please.") Finally, hunger and reason prevailed. If all those people were ordering it, it couldn't be *that* bad. So I called the waitress over and ordered a Kitsune soba for myself. A few minutes later, much to my surprise and relief, a steaming bowl of buckwheat noodles arrived, topped not with filet of fox, but with a lightly sweet and golden bean curd omelet. It was delicious and I ate it with relish.

Feeling somewhat abashed but well fueled with a hearty lunch, we visited the Great Buddha at Todai-ji and walked the path of ten thousand stone lanterns up to the Kasuga Shrine. It was an uplifting and enlightening afternoon, one that I will always remember, especially whenever I eat soba.

We returned to Tokyo, refreshed and ready to resume our teaching. I took the first opportunity to inquire of my students about the mystery of Kitsune soba. They were amused at my naiveté and gladly furnished me with answers.

The fox is an indigenous, if not notorious creature in Japan. It is believed to have the power to bewitch or possess the spirit of anyone who looks into its eyes. It is also the patron of business.

Stone images of foxes can be seen guarding almost every temple, great or small, in Japan. The golden bean curd omelet is called *aburage* (pronounced ah-boo-rah-gay) and is often placed upon the altars of the temples as an offering to the gods who reside there. Foxes are fond of aburage and are said to steal into the temples under the cover of darkness to whisk away the tasty fare left there for them. And thus, this bewitching bit of lore gives Kitsune soba its name.

So, if your travels include a visit to Kyoto and the surrounding countryside, stop to enjoy its beauty and its spirit. And when your appetite beckons, do step into a nearby soba shop and treat yourself to a bowl of *You-Know-What.* ❖

Friends for Life

Just to the north of Kyoto, there's a little village called Ohara, and after making the pilgrimage to all the famous temples of Kyoto, we retired there for a little quiet repose and a soak in a local *onsen*.

Chatani Onsen is a comfortable, unpretentious little inn with *tatami* rooms, shared baths, and a communal dining room. After a day of walking wooded paths along the river for visits to the ancient temple of Jakko-in, the transcendentally beautiful garden of Hosen-in, and the sacred serenity of Sanzen-in, we returned to Chatani for a late afternoon dip in the hot pools. Afterwards, we put on cotton *yukata*, provided by the inn, and went down to the dining room for *shokuji*, a Japanese-style dinner.

We were seated across from each other at a long, low table just inside the entrance of the dining room, with a quiet couple on one side, and a family of seven on the other. Dinner included all the trimmings, from *miso* soup and green salad, to fresh broiled fish with rice and local vegetables. We shared a cold beer with dinner and sat idling over after-dinner conversation and hot *sake*, when the youngest member of the family next to us came toddling over to our table. She was a perfectly beautiful little Japanese girl, not quite two years old, and dressed in her own little *yukata*. She walked right up to me and made herself at home, as if she'd known me all her life. At this, I looked over at her mother and said, "*Kawaii*," to complement her on how cute her daughter was. That comment opened the gateway to conversation and we soon found ourselves chatting away with the Shimizu family.

They were from the city of Kofu in the foothills of Mt. Fuji in the grape-growing region of Yamanashi Prefecture. Masaki, the husband and father, was a doctor and owner of a small family medical clinic. Yuko, his wife, was mother to five beautiful children: Hiroki, the eldest boy, Takae, the eldest girl, Hideki, the younger boy, Toshie, the younger girl, and Ma-chan, the adorable toddler who had wandered up to our table.

We talked with the Shimizu family in the dining room until it became obvious that the proprietors wanted to close up for the night. So we bade each other *Oyasumi nasai*, and agreed to meet there again for breakfast. Alas, the Shimizu were on their way back to Kofu and we were unable to spend the day together. After breakfast, we said goodbye in the lobby and exchanged phone numbers, along with an open invitation from Yuko to visit them at their home in Kofu anytime. And the last thing before they departed, Yuko asked, "By the way, what is your name?" She had invited us to stay at her home before she even knew our names. Only in Japan...

Not only did we take them up on the offer, we became regulars in the Shimizu household, dashing away from the din of Tokyo at every opportunity for a quiet weekend in Kofu. Their hospitality was always relaxed and gracious, and by the time Willie was born, the Shimizu house was like a second home. And since I couldn't be with my own mother, Yuko rose to the occasion and stepped in as my motherhood mentor and Willie's Japanese *Oka-san*. To this day, our two families remain friends, and have continued to enjoy many opportunities over the years to visit each other's homes. The Shimizu house is truly our home away from home in Japan, all because one curious little girl wandered up to me in an *onsen* in Ohara to say hello. ❖

The Song of the Cicada

In Japanese, they're called *semi*, and on muggy summer afternoons, or sometimes just at dusk, you can hear the treetops abuzz with the song of the cicada. It begins with a low-pitched drone, which rises to a deafening crescendo, filling the air of the urban cityscapes and the rural landscapes with the sound of summer.

Much like mayflies, which live for only a single day, cicada live for just a few weeks, during which they take wing, sing their lovesong, find a mate, lay eggs and die. They lay their eggs by making slits in the stems of foliage, where they hatch into tiny wingless creatures called *nymphs*. The nymphs fall to earth and burrow underground to pierce the root of the plant with a needle-like stylet through which they suck its sap for nourishment. Cicada spend many years underground, some species as few as six, others as long as seventeen, where they shed their skins several times before emerging from the earth in the late spring or early summer as adult cicada. Once above ground, leaving the last empty nymph skin behind, they crawl fully-winged into nearby trees.

The males soon burst into song, primarily to attract their mates, but also in groups to repel predatory birds with high-pitched vibrations, which they produce with a rapidly undulating membrane on the abdomen. The sound is so loud and so intense that it can inflict damage to the eardrum at close range.

To some, the familiar drone of the cicada is the first harbinger of the warm season to come, and is oft romanticized in Japanese literature and *haiku*. To others, the sound is maddening; capable of intensifying the heat and ratcheting up the angst in an already tense moment. But there's one thing for sure: It isn't summer in Japan without the song of the cicada. ❖

Kanazawa

It was the pinnacle of summer and we'd been on the road for
several days, stopping off at the famous castle in Matsumoto
on our way to the western prefecture of Ishikawa on the Sea of
Japan to visit Kanazawa, a city famed for its excellent seafood,
its fine lacquerware, and its exquisite gardens.

A Japanese garden is evaluated according to six attributes: The
vastness of its size, the tranquility of its location, the abundance
of moving water, the beauty of its views, the artfulness of its
design, and its endurance over time. Rivaled only by Korakuen
and Kairakuen, the garden of Kenrokuen in Kanazawa is
regarded among the three most beautiful in Japan.

For reasons I can no longer remember, perhaps from too many
uninterrupted hours together, or perhaps from something more
significant, the day that we visited Kenrokuen, Mark and I
were angry at each other. By the time we arrived at the famed
garden, the tension between us was palpable, yet we paid our
entrance fees and went in anyway. But there was no hope
of reconciliation between us that day, and after walking the
manicured paths for most of an hour, we erupted into an
argument at the site of one of the garden's most idyllic views.
Overhead, in the growing heat and humidity of the day, the

cicada droned and buzzed, heightening the drama of our impasse. That's when I knew I had to be alone for a while. As a peace offering, Mark pointed me in the direction of a kimono factory, where the bolts of silk used to make the garments are hand painted on the premises. Since I have both art and tailoring in my blood, watching the serene silk painters behind a glass display window, precisely and patiently creating opulent floral patterns on yard after yard of silk, was the perfect antidote for the morning's anger and frustration. After watching them paint for more than an hour, I toured the factory and bought a tiny silk coin purse made from the scraps of a hand-sewn kimono as a souvenir.

The locale of the kimono factory offered no other attractions, and its utilitarian streets were bereft of other shops and storefronts, so I turned my path back to Kenrokuen. After all, it was my one and only chance to enjoy its beauty, and perhaps I could appreciate it now that I was on my own. I made my way back to the gates of the garden, but instead of going in through the main entrance, I entered somehow through a smaller gate in a remote corner of the grounds.

Just inside, I found a small, humble, very old Buddhist temple. With the discord of the day still thrashing around in my head, I sat down on the low stone wall that surrounded it, to study it in detail and bask in its tranquility. The temple was so old that almost all of the original paint had been worn away, down to the bare wood. As I sat there on the steps of that temple, somehow, in those few moments, I was able to put my feelings into perspective, to realize that they were insignificant and meaningless in the grand scheme of things. A hundred years from now, who would be there to care? Not even me.

Kanazawa

All at once, I felt an overwhelming sense of relief and resolve. I was ready to move on. I rose from the stone wall and headed off to enjoy the beauty of the garden. Kenrokuen exceeded all promises and expectations: An exquisite marriage of man and nature, a divine consummation of heaven and earth.

Afterwards, when I returned to our lodgings, Mark still had not returned. Oddly I was glad, because I was in the mood to write something about the day. So, after a soothing soak in the *furo*, I donned a fresh *yukata* and settled down on the *tatami* at a low table and wrote an essay entitled *Upon Walking Away From a Buddhist Temple.* ❖

Upon Walking Away From a Buddhist Temple

O Ancient Temple! As I sit upon your timeworn stairs today, wrapped in thought, obsessed with mood, contemplating the insignificant, somewhere in my bones I know that, as you stood here in all your humble splendor long before me, you will continue to stand here long after I and all my petty problems and dramas have ceased to exist. When I am no longer alive to create them, they and I will vanish; but you will not. Not yet.

You will stand; perhaps more rounded at your corners and edges, perhaps less colorful, as the blasts of winter and the merciless scorch of summer nibble and eke at the brilliant hues which once dazzled upon your sturdy planks and carven eaves. You are timeless. You are time itself; built of wood that does not decay, and of stone indestructible, by the hands of a faith that does not waver.

Who am I little I? To sit upon your wizened stones, daring to disregard all that you are; engaging instead in brooding over the menial dialogues that ricochet in my thoughts like misdirected mantras. Where is thy peace, and thus mine? Show me, in your sentient silence, how to reconcile the profound

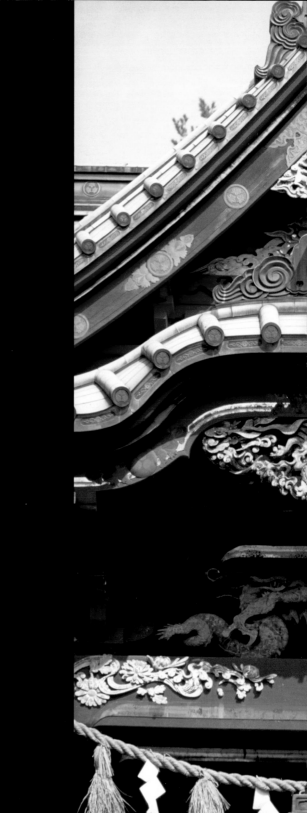

with the profane. How do I maintain my lofty idealism amid
the random chaos of the world at large?

I come to you today with spinning head: a paradox of acceptance
and intolerance. My thoughts are rife with the full spectrum of
nuance, from prejudice to pity, from humor to horror, from
sentiment to sarcasm, from rebellion to resolve. The world is
too much with me, and I brought it all to your sanctum.

Yet, as I feel your stones in my bones, I know I shall rise and
walk away; perhaps more rounded at my corners and edges,
perhaps less adamant as life and time nibble and eke at my
carven ideals. But like you, I shall stand, built by the hand of
a faith that does not waver. ❖

Tick Tock...Drip Drop

On our last day in the city of Kanazawa, I wandered downtown by myself for a bite of lunch. On my outing, I discovered that, in conjunction with its historical elements, much of downtown Kanazawa is quite modern, with stylish architecture, chic boutiques and savvy businesses. After a tasty meal in a Chinese luncheonette, I stepped out into the sunshine to do a bit of exploring. In a little plaza, not far from the restaurant where I had eaten, I discovered an amazing little treasure: One of Bernard Gitton's water clocks!

Of course, at the time, I'd never heard of Bernard Gitton or his magical clocks. But through later research, I learned that he is a French physicist and artist who, after leaving the world of scientific research in 1979, now creates water clocks, water calculators, fountains, and other scientific works of art in a studio that was once an eleventh-century church on the Loire River.

Gitton calls his works *Horloges a Voir le Temps Couler*: Time Flow Clocks. These delightful contraptions are composed of a complex assembly of hand-blown glass bubbles, beakers, burettes, and pipettes, filled with a mixture of colored water and methyl alcohol. They function on the basic principles of gravity and hydraulics, in which the liquid begins in a large reservoir from which it drips, second by second, into a little tumbler, which, when full, tips its contents into a series of tubes leading to a graduated vertical measuring chamber that marks each minute as it fills. Once full, the chamber empties itself automatically into the "hour" glass, and the process starts all over again.

With precision that rivals a Swiss watch, Gitton's water clocks keep time in cities around the world, including Amsterdam, Andorra La Vella, Berlin, Cascaïs-Lisboa, Copenhagen, Geneva, Indianapolis, Innsbruck, Jakarta, La Hague, Le Tampon, London, Mallièvre, New York, Oviedo, Papeete, Paris, Porto Alegre, Rio de Janeiro, Rockford, São Paulo, Seoul, and Vancouver.

Japan appears to be the biggest market for Gitton's clocks, which can be seen in Ashikaga, Hiratsuka, Kakogawa, Kyushu, Nagoya, Okayama, Osaka, Tokuyama, Yanai, and Yokohama. Imagine my surprise when I discovered that two of his wondrous clocks were right in my back yard: One stands at the IBM Building in Tokyo, and the other, in my beloved Yamanashi. How on earth could I have missed them? Perhaps the cosmos was saving the moment for that afternoon in Kanazawa.

It was about twenty minutes to three when I first laid eyes on the clock. I was mystified at first, and it took me a few minutes to figure out what it was. But once I did, I was so captivated by its ingenuity and precision that I felt compelled to watch until it reached the top of the hour, just to see what would happen. I was enchanted as I followed the progress of the blue liquid from one chamber to the next, checking my watch every few minutes to verify its precision. Right on time. When the stroke of three finally arrived, the magical structure tumbled its contents into the hour chamber and began filling itself all over again, drop by drop. At that, I continued on my way, with a smile of delight that returns to my face every time I recall Monsieur Gitton's wonderful water clock. ❖

Wajima

On Honshu's west central shore, on the Sea of Japan, at the very tip of the Noto Peninsula, all the way out at land's end, is the lovely hamlet of Wajima. It's a quiet little town overlooking a fisherman's wharf, and on any given day, to the casual observer, not much appears to be happening in Wajima. But while tourists like us were browsing in shops and enjoying culinary delicacies, hundreds of artisans were hard at work, making Japan's finest lacquerware. Early in the mornings, there's an open-air market called the *Asa-ichi*, where local merchants, most of whom are ladies dressed in traditional garments, peddle their goods and fresh produce on tented mats on the ground. Throughout the year, Wajima is also the site of many traditional festivals.

Our two-day stay in Wajima was all too brief, but we had the good fortune to find the best lodgings of any place we stayed in all of Japan. The inn was an old wooden building, and from the street, it appeared quite unremarkable. But once inside, the *genkan* where guests remove their shoes revealed a quadrangle of traditional rooms overlooking a small garden in the center. Ours was an especially large room on the upper story, with expansive *tatami* floors, lots of extra futons and pillows, and large window screens that could be propped open with a stick for a view of the garden below.

The proprietor was a quietly gracious young woman named Yuko who spoke good English for someone so far out in the provinces. Yet something in her demeanor betrayed a hint of sardonic wistfulness. Something unfulfilled or unrequited. In little snippets of conversation with Yuko over the next couple of days, I learned that at nearly thirty, she was still unmarried, and had resigned herself to spending the rest of her days running the family business with her aging mother. To her, it seemed as if she would be stuck in that little town forever…a tender trap indeed.

On the last evening in Wajima, we donned our *yukata* and walked down to the beach to witness a *taiko* drumming performance that had originally been a means of frightening away invading enemies. I must admit that, as we sat there in the firelight on the dark beach, the drummer in his gruesome mask and wild headdress, and the *toom-toom-tum* of the great *taiko* drum, were very intimidating. Afterwards, the spectators, most of them dressed in *yukata*, with wooden *geta* on their feet, made a mass exit toward home. The rattle of hundreds of *geta*, clicking and clogging along the streets of Wajima is a sound effect that still echoes in my memory.

The following morning, we enjoyed a traditional breakfast of *miso* soup, pickled salad, dried fish and white rice. Afterwards, as we bade a reluctant farewell to Yuko, the fleeting thought crossed my mind that I could be quite happy living her life there in Wajima. And in that same moment, something in her eyes told me that she would gladly have traded places. ❖

Onegaishimasu

When you travel deep into the heart of the island of Honshu, the sophisticated trappings of Tokyo fall away with each passing kilometer, and the Japanese people emerge in their purest form. To a foreigner traveling in the quaint region of Fukushima Prefecture, this can be both a blessing and a curse.

We arrived in the historic village of Aizu Wakamatsu late one afternoon during a particularly busy holiday season. Japan has an excellent network of tourist bureaus, and as was often our habit, we had waited until we were there to make arrangements for our lodgings. We were met at the tourist bureau by Toshiko, a friendly and capable young woman who was eager to help us find a place to spend the night.

We were Toshiko's last customers of the day and she gave us her undivided attention as she began making telephone calls to nearby inns. Meanwhile, we browsed around the tourist office, which was beautifully decorated with photographs, artifacts and local crafts, until we began to realize that something was terribly wrong. Toshiko was on her fifth or sixth phone call and still had found no lodgings for us.

The tension became increasingly audible in her voice as she made the eighth, ninth, and tenth attempts. Based on the half of the conversations that I could hear, and what little Japanese I could understand, it seemed that none of the proprietors of the inns she contacted were willing to put up a couple of foreigners for the night. I managed to infer from a comprehensible word here and there, that they thought foreigners were too fussy. Foreigners didn't know that they were supposed to remove their shoes, they couldn't use chopsticks, they couldn't get used to Japanese toilets, and didn't like sleeping on the floor. Some innkeepers simply didn't allow *gaijin* to stay in their establishments.

Long after Toshiko should have closed up for the night and gone home, she was still on the phone, trying to find an inn that would take us. But by now, she was down on her knees, and her polite cajoling had given way to a desperate flood of tears as she sobbed her plea of *Onegaishimasu* into the telephone receiver. Still, no one was willing to take us in. We were beginning to entertain the notion of sleeping at the train station or on a park bench, when at long last, after calls to no fewer than two dozen inns, Toshiko finally succeeded. Somewhere in the village of Aizu Wakamatsu, she had found the only innkeeper who would open her doors to a couple of weary America-*jin*. And as if that weren't enough, Toshiko drove us there in her own car.

Having grown up in Alabama, amid the racial tensions of the Deep South, I witnessed firsthand the kinds of insults and cruelty that people can inflict upon each other. And although I can honestly say that I have never engaged in racist epithets or exclusionary prejudice, until that day in Aizu Wakamatsu, I had never been on the receiving end of it either.

The inn exceeded our now modest expectations. It was nicely kept, the evening meal was delicious and elegantly served, the futons were clean and comfortable, and to our added delight, the innkeeper and her daughters actually took a liking to us. After the dinner dishes were cleared away, we spent the rest of the evening chatting with them, and even took a group photo to commemorate the occasion. It was an uplifting end to an otherwise disappointing day, and that kindly innkeeper single-handedly restored my faith in the people of rural Japan. ✤

A Moment In History

Emperor Hirohito died while I was in Japan. Actually, that's not entirely true. I was on vacation in Hawaii when he died on the seventh of January. We touched down at Narita early in the morning of January eighth, and there had been no mention of it on the plane or on the train back to Tokyo. It wasn't until we arrived home and turned on the television that news of the Emperor's death reached us.

It came as no shock however, as we had been watching him slowly dying, little by little, day by day, for many months. His gradual decline had begun the previous summer, with reports that the Emperor was being treated for some sort of gastric disorder, but it was soon disclosed that he was hemorrhaging in the duodenum between his stomach and small intestine. Every day thereafter, newspaper articles and televised reports informed the public of every minute detail of the Emperor's condition. They disclosed his vital statistics: his heart rate, his blood pressure, his weight, his temperature, and how many times he breathed each minute. They published a running tally of how many cc's of blood he had lost and how much had been replaced through transfusions. They reported on his disposition, his daily activities, and exactly what he ate at every meal. And each day, it was a little less optimistic, a little more grim.

One news story at a time, we watched him fade away, although we were never actually allowed to see him. He had long since ceased making public appearances. However, each evening, after the day's last television broadcast had finished, a live cam image of the outside of the Imperial Palace would fill the screen, while classical music played in the background. Sometimes I would leave it on while I read or studied Japanese. It was soothing and comforting. It made me feel somehow connected. And after many weeks of watching the familiar scene where Japan's beloved Emperor lay dying, the image of the stone bridge arching over a moat protecting the secluded palace lives on in my memory. ❖

Somewhere Over the Rainbow

If anyone had told me at age twenty-one that, twelve years later, I would have a baby in Japan, I'd have had a good laugh and told them that they were quite crazy. But that's exactly what happened. Of course, having a baby in Japan wasn't in the original plan, but then destiny never pays much heed to the small devices of us mortals.

When I first suspected that I was pregnant, I lived in denial for weeks. During our winter vacation in Hawaii, I told myself that the fact that I didn't look so hot in a bikini anymore was just a symptom of spending my days with my bottom planted in chair all day, and a few too many Japanese sweet cakes. But after the third month, I took a "sick day" from work and went to the American Clinic across from the Tokyo Tower. It was there that I finally admitted to myself what I already knew. I was pregnant.

On the way back home, I was so dazed by the notion that I got all the way to Senkawa Station on the Yurakucho Line before I realized that I had completely missed my stop at Ikebukuro. By now it was evening and time to face the music. When I arrived home, I took out a piece of red origami paper.

On it I drew a big heart, and inside the heart I wrote the words, "When does 1+1=3?" I taped it to the front door and waited.

That evening, Mark and I decided to stay and have the baby in Japan. In honor of the upcoming event, on the first day of May, while vacationing in Tochigi Prefecture, we got married at the ward office in the lovely alpine town of Nikko. Later that summer, we revisited the Dai Butsu at Kamakura, and this time, through a little hatch door at the back, I went down into the belly of the great statue. To be standing inside the belly of the Buddha, with my baby stirring in my own, was a truly blessed moment.

My pregnancy was idyllic, with no morning sickness or other discomfort, and I continued teaching until my eighth month. I grew quite rotund in those last weeks, especially when the baby didn't arrive on schedule. Fourteen anxious days later, on August 28th, I awoke in a puddle at six a.m. and realized that my water had broken. I was in labor. With my contractions coming about thirty minutes apart, we calmly got dressed and walked down to the corner to hail a taxi to take us to Seibo Byoin, a nearby Catholic hospital.

We spent the afternoon in a comfortable private room, with my contractions growing steadily closer and closer together.

The hospital provided me with my own private midwife, who coached me through every breath. By the time my contractions were less than five minutes apart, I thought that they would drive me mad. It's not that I was in any great pain per se, it's just that there was never enough time to rest in between. The midwife recommended that I choose an object and focus on it while I breathed through each one.

There was a small window above my hospital bed, and at about five p.m., after I'd focused on every object in the room, and breathed through what seemed like a thousand contractions, I turned toward that window and fixed my gaze on the Tokyo skyline. And that's when I saw it: The biggest, brightest, most glorious rainbow I'd ever seen, arching radiantly over the city.

At 6:22 p.m., the moment finally came when I held my baby boy in my arms and looked into his eyes for the first time. I can say without hesitation that it was the greatest moment of my life. He was perfect in every way: healthy, beautiful, and pure as a dewdrop. We named him Will. Not for William, but for a concept conceived by Kurt Vonnegut in his novel *The Sirens of Titan*, known as *The Universal Will To Become*. ❖

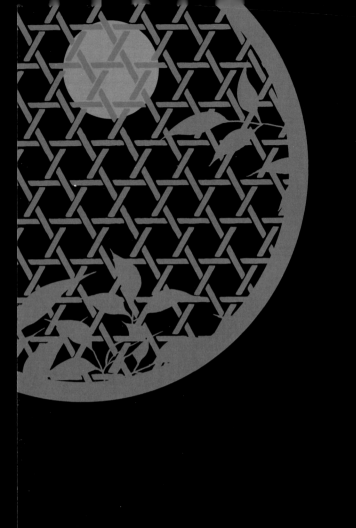

Above and Beyond

Giving birth to Will was one of the most exhilarating experiences of my life. It took only twelve hours and was blessedly uncomplicated. It was all natural, with no drugs or incision, and the team of doctors and nurses were both kind and competent. I am often fond of saying that if ever I decided to have another baby, I would go back to Japan for the birth.

They let me hold him for a long time afterwards before moving him to the nursery for the night. I was loath to part with him after waiting so long and working so hard on his arrival, but mother and baby were both exhausted, and it was probably best that we go our separate ways to get some much-needed rest.

I was still flying high on my own adrenalin and endorphins when the nurse moved me to the six-bed maternity ward. She made me comfortable and offered me a little blue pill that she said would help me sleep. Instead of taking it, I tucked it into the pocket of my pajamas. I wasn't ready to fall asleep yet. I wanted to relive the moment of my son's birth a few more times in my head before I called it a night. The nurse drew the curtains around my bed and wished me *oyasumi nasai*.

As I lay there in the white cocoon of my hospital bed, I could picture each and every moment of the day with the clarity of a

Technicolor movie. I watched it over and over again in my mind's eye until midnight when the night nurse came by to check the ward. When she found me still awake, she asked why I hadn't taken the pill and whether I was having trouble sleeping. I explained to her that I was too excited to sleep and just wanted to enjoy the moment.

When she came around the second time at two a.m. and found me again still awake, she was concerned that I would be too tired in the morning when time came to visit the nursery for the morning's first feeding. I still didn't want to take the sedative, and she didn't insist. Instead, she sweetly offered to help me relax by rubbing my *feet* until I fell asleep. As tempting as it sounded, I couldn't with any conscience allow her to spoil me in such an indulgent way. So I thanked her politely for the offer, pointing out that she must be very busy with her nightly duties. I assured her that I would be fine and wished her *oyasumi nasai*. Eventually, I did fall asleep that night, thinking to myself as I drifted off, "Only in Japan..." ✥

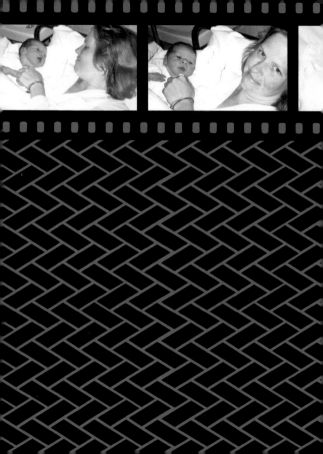

Seibo Byoin

Will was born in the Tokyo suburb of Mejiro, at the International Catholic Hospital known as Seibo Byoin, a name that means *Mother of Peace*. At five a.m. on the first morning of Will's new life, I was awakened by a gentle chime emanating from the maternity ward's speaker system, along with a message in Japanese that essentially said it was time for all mothers to wake up and go to the nursery to feed their babies. I'd been awake with excitement nearly all night and was still a little groggy, but I was soon filled with the same excitement I'd felt the night before, and couldn't wait to hold my baby in my arms again. The other mothers ambled sluggishly down the corridor behind me, so I was first in line outside the nursery door.

There were fifty-two babies in the Seibo nursery the day that Will was born, and Will made fifty-three. As a precaution, all mothers and babies are required to wear red medallions with matching numbers on them around their wrists, and each mother must present her medallion at the nursery door to avoid a potential mother-baby mix-up. And although there was no mistaking Will as the one that belonged to me, I had to show my medallion anyway.

Will wasn't the only foreign baby however. There were two others. Twins. They had been born prematurely; the boy at

750 grams, and the girl at 600, and they were still in incubators. But by the time Will arrived, they were already several months old, and had grown fat and roly-poly. They were beautiful and exotic, as their parents were natives of Nairobi. In days to come, I would often see them wearing their native garb when they came to visit the twins.

But as unique and adorable as they were, the Kenyan babies were old news. Will was the new celebrity. All the nurses wanted to hold him, and to help me with him, so I had plenty of coaching for his first feeding. But once the nurses had briefed me on the fine points of breastfeeding, they went on their way to help the other mothers and left us alone to share that special moment. And as I looked down at my newborn son cradled in my arms, I felt a joy and fulfillment that only a mother can know, and I now understood why they call it *Seibo Byoin*. ❖

Cats

I've always been a cat lover. But up until the day I moved into 101 Ikebukuro Flat, I had only been acquainted with the domestic variety, the ones that we spoil, pamper, and dote upon back home. I was delighted at first to discover a small colony of cats living in the alleyway next to our apartment, and I immediately envisioned myself adopting one of them, giving it a name, and gradually coaxing it inside to become a devoted pet. Boy was I dreaming.

The first night I went out there with a saucer of milk, which, by the way, cost an emperor's ransom at the corner market, I got a startling lesson on how the other half lives. I soon learned that these were no pedigreed felines like the ones in T.S. Eliot's *Old Possum's Book of Practical Cats*. In fact, the mangiest, orneriest stray from back home would easily have won best of show in this bunch. But names like Growltiger, Griddlebone, Mungojerrie, Rumpleteazer, Mistoffelees, Macavity, and Skimbleshanks would have suited them splendidly.

They scattered in all directions when I approached them, but nevertheless, I was determined to surprise them with a nourishing treat. When I knelt down on the ground to offer it to them, they instantly formed a ring around me, hungrily eyeing the single saucer of milk I'd brought for them to share. But instead of meowing and rubbing up against me like most cats I knew, they hissed at me and bared their teeth as if they'd just stepped out of the jungle. Terrified that they would leap on me and disfigure my face or infect me with rabies, I thrust the saucer of milk into the midst of the rabble and bolted for the safety of my apartment. After that, I still fed them from time to time, but only with bits of kitchen scraps that I tossed hastily onto the pavement when I went to take out the garbage.

However, there was one that stood out from the group. She was an orange and white calico, starved so thin that she looked like an anatomical model of a cat skeleton with fur on it. I'd been watching her since she was a kitten, and around the time I first became pregnant with Will, she began jumping the garden wall and showing up at the back door, and I couldn't resist slipping her a bite of meat or a sip of milk when she did. She was different from the others, not quite so feral and distant. Still she was filthy and infested with fleas, so I didn't dare touch her or invite her in. It wasn't long however, before I noticed that she too was pregnant. Despite her emaciated condition, the conspicuous bulge in her tummy left no room for doubt.

Day by day, I watched as she grew rounder. Of course, my own pregnancy wasn't progressing nearly as rapidly, and when she

disappeared for a couple of days, I knew that she must have gone off somewhere to have her kittens. Sure enough, after a few days, she showed up begging at my back door, looking as lean as ever. I spotted her kittens a few weeks later, roaming about with the other cats in the alleyway. At first, I was tempted to kidnap one of them and domesticate it before it could adopt the wild ways of the alley, but with a baby on the way, it hardly seemed wise.

Throughout that spring and summer, the months of my pregnancy passed one by one, and the skinny orange and white calico continued show up at my back door every day for a morsel to eat. I was just into my eighth month and getting quite rotund when I noticed that my little backdoor beggar was also pregnant...again. The gestation period for cats is only sixty days, but still I was amazed that it had happened so soon. Then I began to wonder if it was possible that she would deliver not one but two litters of kittens before my due date. And so, the race was on.

I watched her every day for the next two months, growing round again, her ripening belly wagging beneath her bony ribs and hips. I too was close, anxiously ticking days off of the calendar and waiting for my water to break. But my due date came and went. Will was late. Meanwhile, my feline rival had disappeared again, and there was still no sign of her the day I checked into Seibo Byoin. But five days later, when I returned home with my bundle of joy, she was waiting at the back door for me, and a half-dozen new kitties were roaming playfully about in the alley. I couldn't believe my eyes. My calico mama had beaten me to the finish line…twice! ✤

Oyayubi

Japan is a culture with many superstitions, especially surrounding death and the funereal ceremony that follows. Japanese funerals are highly stylized rites, conducted by Buddhist priests according to the traditions of the Buddhist religion. A wake is held for the deceased, during which friends and family come to pay their respects. A special meal is served, and afterwards, the immediate family and close friends accompany the body of the deceased to the crematorium.

Many symbolic rituals are performed during the mourning process. For purification, a small mound of salt is placed on the threshold of the home of the deceased. In some cases, after cremation, family members use chopsticks to pass the charred remains of the deceased from person to person, until they are placed at last in the crematory urn for burial. An offering of food is often placed on the graves of the deceased, with a pair of chopsticks standing upright in it.

One of the strangest superstitions associated with the funeral ceremony is the practice of hiding one's thumbs by wrapping the other fingers around them whenever a funeral procession passes by. The Japanese word for thumb is *oyayubi*, which, when literally translated, means "parent finger." According to Japanese superstition, if you happen to see a funeral procession passing by and you forget to hide your thumbs, you will not be present to comfort your parents when they die.

My father died while I was in Japan. I knew that he was ill, and for that reason I paid a farewell visit to my hometown to see him one more time before I left for Tokyo. I'll never forget him standing in the doorway of my childhood home, waving goodbye. I didn't know it then, but that would be the last time I ever saw him.

About three months after my son was born, I was beginning to feel like myself again, and the prospect of making the trip home to see my parents didn't seem so impossible anymore. One evening, I decided that I was ready to bring my baby home to meet them, so I hopped on my bicycle and headed over to the Hotel Metropolitan to use the international pay telephone. When I called my parents' house to tell them the good news, my older sister answered the phone, and I immediately asked how my father was doing. After a short but dreadful pause, she said, "Oh no, you don't know..." She gave the phone to my mother, who tearfully told me that my father had died ten days earlier, and had already been buried. In that instant, all joy was extinguished.

It seems that our nameplate had fallen off the mailbox, and when the Western Union deliveryman came with the telegram, he couldn't figure out which apartment was ours, so he left without delivering it. I didn't learn of my father's death until that fateful evening almost two weeks later. Such a cruel twist of fate. Much of my memory after that is a blur, but somehow I remember thinking on the long ride home, that I must have forgotten to hide my thumbs. ❖

Sayonara

Every foreigner who has ever lived in Japan realizes at some point that it's time to go. We all have our reasons. After the death of my father, I fell into a deep depression, and one day, while vacantly watching particles of dust dance on a beam of sunlight over a cup of tea in the *tatami* room, I knew that going home would be my only salvation. So I bought myself a one-way ticket to San Francisco, packed up my baby and my belongings and bade farewell to the life that I had so loved in Tokyo. It was one of the most difficult decisions I have ever made.

After a short stopover in California, I spent the next three months at my parents' house in my hometown of Mobile, Alabama with Will. It was strange to be back in the States again after all that had happened, and all that time in Japan. But it was comforting too, to be among close family and old friends once again. Finally, after weeks of coming to grips with the reality of his death, one summer afternoon, I visited the cemetery and planted a dogwood tree on my father's grave.

Over time, I found joy again. Upon my return to the Napa Valley, I became a private tutor to the children of Japan Airlines flight instructors living with their families in the U.S. My son has grown into a brilliant young man, and has even returned to Japan for a visit to his birthplace. I still miss my father every day, and I miss Japan just as often. But life is good, and Japan will still be there in all its grace and splendor when I am ready to return. ❖

Back to His Beginnings

Fast-forward ten years, to July 7, the day Will embarked on a visit to Japan with his father. I was a chaos of emotion at the prospect of letting him go…halfway around the planet…for five weeks. At the same time, the idea of him going with his father to visit all the places in Japan that I cherish so dearly was the opportunity of a lifetime. I had to let him go.

In the weeks before his departure, I helped Will prepare for the trip by assembling a waist pack of travel supplies, with an ID card, a few Band-Aids, a package of tissues, some Japanese coins, and a pocket dictionary. And just so he'd know what kind of culture shock awaited him on the other side of the Pacific, we also reveled in the humor of *Dave Barry Does Japan*, which Will read aloud to me in its entirety.

Meanwhile, his father, who is quite techno-savvy, worked with me to set up an online communication system so that we could keep in touch via the Internet throughout their trip. We downloaded software for international long distance through our computer modems, we installed an instant message chat program so that we could type at each other in real time, and signed up for space on a web-based file storage site where I would be able to view digital photos of their adventures.

There was a monster of a typhoon brewing over the Pacific the day that Will and Mark left LAX bound for Narita Airport. Knowing that I wouldn't have a moment's peace until I'd heard from them, I turned once again to the World Wide Web for a solution. I logged onto a website that allowed me to monitor their flight, mile by mile, complete with the flight plan, altitude, airspeed, distance traveled, distance remaining, and estimated arrival time. I watched in wonder as I tracked my precious boy all the way across the Pacific Ocean, and breathed deep sigh of relief when the website indicated that their flight had arrived safely. A few hours later, when my telephone rang, I heard the sweet sound of Will's voice on the other end, calling from the *tatami* family room that I knew so well in the Shimizu house in Kofu. Willie had arrived at his home away from home and was now in the loving care of Yuko Shimizu, his Japanese *oka-san*.

For the next five weeks, I chatted with Will at pre-arranged times via instant message on the Internet, and we were occasionally able to connect for live voice conversations by phone or by using the international dial-up software, although that method was never very successful or satisfying. But best of all, each day, I logged onto the file storage website, downloaded digital photos of the day's activities and experienced a virtual vacation with Will.

I saw him playing with the Shimizu children in the *tatami* family room. I saw him waiting to board the *Shinkansen* at Tokyo Station. I saw him swimming in the Sea of Japan, wearing a *yukata* in a Japanese *minshuku* in Wajima, playing *mah jongg* with our neighbor Takeda-san, grinning at me from the slopes of Mt. Fuji, peering out from the belly of the Great Buddha at Kamakura; and best of all, at Seibo Byoin, standing in front of the delivery room where he was born.

Looking at all those pictures of Will, having the time of his life in all my favorite places in Japan was almost as good as being there. But nothing compared with the joy of wrapping my arms around him and kissing his sweet face the day that he returned. Next time...I'm going with him. ❖

Being There

By Will Raus

For years I had been longing to go to Japan. I was born in Tokyo, and I had seen my mother's pictures of Japan many times. But even though I had looked at photographs of all those places that I knew were such an important part of my life, I could not truly feel what Japan meant to me. Not until I could actually feel it by being there, by returning to the place where I was born.

My father and I left from LAX Airport on July 7, ready for the 12-hour flight from Los Angeles to Narita Airport near Tokyo. When we arrived, we found our friend Yuko Shimizu waiting for us the instant we got off the plane. Once we'd made it through the unloading gates, we headed out to the car for the one and a half hour trip to the Shimizu home in Kofu. Our Japan adventure had begun.

Over the next five weeks, we took so many trips to different places in Japan that I can't even remember them all. We took a cruise around Yokohama Bay, we visited Lake Hakone, we went trout fishing in the foothills of Mt. Fuji, we rode the Japanese Bullet Train to the city of Kyoto, we watched summer fireworks from a hillside temple in Kofu, and we spent our last day in Japan at Tokyo Disneyland.

One of our most significant trips was to the city of Kamakura to visit the Taiisan Kotokuin Shojo Shrine, the home of one of the largest statues of Buddha in the world. It is said that the great Buddha once stood inside a building, but when the building was washed away by a *tsunami*, the statue was left standing. The Taiisan Kotokuin Shojo Shrine is my mother's favorite place in the whole world, and in pictures, I had seen her standing in front of the statue of the great Buddha while she was pregnant with me. But until I saw it for myself, I had not actually been able to feel its effect on me. Even if I hadn't had any personal connection with it, the Buddha itself would have been magnificent. But knowing that I had been down inside its belly before I was even born, made it that much more special.

Every country has its center of commerce, and Tokyo is one of the world's most impressive examples. But, it somehow manages to combine that metropolitan conglomeration with great cultural beauty. Among the beehive of activity, here and there, quiet gardens radiate peace. The beauty of the gardens doesn't seem to fit with the hustle and bustle of Tokyo, yet they coexist so perfectly.

Tokyo also has many marvels of architecture. As its nickname implies, the Tokyo Dome arches above the city like a Big Egg, and the Sunshine 60 Building shoots up from the skyline like a rocket. And from the top of the Hotel Metropolitan, the city of Tokyo seems to go on forever.

It was on our visit to Tokyo that I finally arrived at the moment I'd been waiting for. After lunch at the Hotel Metropolitan, we took a taxi to Seibo Byoin, the hospital where I was born. At first sight, it looked quite plain and ordinary, nothing at all like I had imagined. Our friend and translator Takeshi Takeoka spoke with a receptionist at the front desk who gave us permission to tour the hospital on our own. We headed straight for the maternity ward where my dad took a picture of me standing in front of the door of the very same delivery room where I was born. At last, I felt like I'd come home.

My father and I also visited the small fishing town of Wajima, in western Japan. Legend has it that, in ancient times, the Chinese attempted an attack on Japan by sea. The people of Wajima assembled on the beach wearing fearsome masks and beating drums to scare away their invaders. A typhoon soon swallowed up the Chinese fleet, and the people of Wajima were saved. But even though the town has such a stormy history, the trip to Wajima was one of our more peaceful adventures in Japan. We visited the morning market, and stopped by the inn where my mother and father had stayed eleven years before. In that town, I found little hustle and bustle. As small towns go, Wajima was a stark contrast to Tokyo. It was a good little place to let go of it all.

Outside the cities, Japan is the green that never ends, with its emerald rice paddies and terraced tea farms. Mt. Fuji towers majestically in the background of almost every landscape. Japan is the most beautiful place I have ever seen. But alas, all good things must come to an end, as does this story.

I cried the day we left Japan, watching out the window of the plane as it rose higher and higher above that beautiful land. I was glad when the mainland disappeared from view, so it wouldn't remind me of how much I missed it already. Those thirty-seven days were some of the best days of my life, and I find myself longing once again for the day when I return home...to Japan. ❖

Photo Acknowledgments

Robert George
Celeste Heiter
Nolan Heiter
Edwin McKelpin
Mark Raus
Will Raus

Celeste Heiter is a 20-year resident of California's beautiful Napa Valley. A native of Mobile, Alabama, she holds a Bachelor of Arts in English and Art from the University of South Alabama. Celeste spent two years teaching English in Tokyo, where her son Will was born. Since her return to the Napa Valley, she has worked as a freelance writer and specialized language instructor for Japanese students attending school in the United States.

Read short stories, articles, interviews and reviews by Celeste Heiter at www.thingsasian.com

The Fox and the Foreigner
The Echo of Ancient Drumbeats
Have Camera, Will Travel
Of Destinations and Dog Biscuits
Prometheus Unbound
The Cycle of Life
and more...

Other ThingsAsian Press books by Celeste Heiter

Ganbatte Means Go For It!
or…How to Become an English
Teacher in Japan
ISBN 0-9715940-0-7
USA $14.95
CAN $25